STARTING A LAW PRACTICE AND PROFESSIONALISM FOR NEW LAWYERS

ASPEN SELECT SERIES

STARTING A LAW PRACTICE AND PROFESSIONALISM FOR NEW LAWYERS

ALEXANDER Y. BENIKOV

About Wolters Kluwer Law & Business

Wolters Kluwer Law & Business is a leading global provider of intelligent information and digital solutions for legal and business professionals in key specialty areas, and respected educational resources for professors and law students. Wolters Kluwer Law & Business connects legal and business professionals as well as those in the education market with timely, specialized authoritative content and information-enabled solutions to support success through productivity, accuracy and mobility.

Serving customers worldwide, Wolters Kluwer Law & Business products include those under the Aspen Publishers, CCH, Kluwer Law International, Loislaw, ftwilliam.com and MediRegs family of products.

CCH products have been a trusted resource since 1913, and are highly regarded resources for legal, securities, antitrust and trade regulation, government contracting, banking, pension, payroll, employment and labor, and healthcare reimbursement and compliance professionals.

Aspen Publishers products provide essential information to attorneys, business professionals and law students. Written by preeminent authorities, the product line offers analytical and practical information in a range of specialty practice areas from securities law and intellectual property to mergers and acquisitions and pension/benefits. Aspen's trusted legal education resources provide professors and students with high-quality, up-to-date and effective resources for successful instruction and study in all areas of the law.

Kluwer Law International products provide the global business community with reliable international legal information in English. Legal practitioners, corporate counsel and business executives around the world rely on Kluwer Law journals, looseleafs, books, and electronic products for comprehensive information in many areas of international legal practice.

Loislaw is a comprehensive online legal research product providing legal content to law firm practitioners of various specializations. Loislaw provides attorneys with the ability to quickly and efficiently find the necessary legal information they need, when and where they need it, by facilitating access to primary law as well as state-specific law, records, forms and treatises.

ftwilliam.com offers employee benefits professionals the highest quality plan documents (retirement, welfare and non-qualified) and government forms (5500/PBGC, 1099 and IRS) software at highly competitive prices.

MediRegs products provide integrated health care compliance content and software solutions for professionals in healthcare, higher education and life sciences, including professionals in accounting, law and consulting.

Wolters Kluwer Law & Business, a division of Wolters Kluwer, is headquartered in New York. Wolters Kluwer is a market-leading global information services company focused on professionals.

For My Parents

TABLE OF CONTENTS

ACKNOWLEDGMENTS

This book would not have been possible without the help of many people. The first person I have to thank is my amazing wife. She supported my dream when few people did. As I told her on our wedding day, she is my role model. I also have to thank my parents. I have to thank them for many things, not the least of which was getting me out of Russia. A big thank you to my whole family is also in order.

A special thank you goes to Burt Burleson, who was my Law Office Management Professor in law school. He was the first person who got me to seriously think about starting my own practice. Without him, I don't know if I would have ever thought about starting my own practice right out of law school. I also have to thank two amazing professors that I was fortunate to have had: Professor Ernie Ettlich and Prakash Chenjeri taught me how to really think, and I will be forever indebted to them.

I also have to thank the many wonderful defense attorneys in Phoenix that took me in under their wings and showed me the ropes and helped me to get on my feet. The one person I have to mention by name is Jesus Acosta. He was my biggest mentor, and I don't know if I would have made it through my first year without his help.

A special thank you has to be said for the students that put in a ton of work editing this book: Joel Brito, Kenneth Davison, Christina Griffin, Steve Miller, Paul Morton, Gordon Nitka, and Darren Richardson all did excellent work. A special thank you goes to Heidi Haru Ernst, who did a lot of work on editing, formatting, and preparing the Index. The last student I must thank is my wonderful intern Melissa Well-Spicer, who did a ton of editing. This book would not have been possible without everyone's help. I must also thank Phoenix School of Law for allowing me to teach and thank my wonderful students for putting up with me.

Chapter 1
From the Bakery
to the Court House

"Life grants nothing to us mortals without hard work" –Horace-

I share my own story throughout this book, not to brag or to talk about myself but to hopefully inspire and to motivate law students and young attorneys. I always tell people that if I can do it, you can too. Success in the legal field is about hard work, sacrifice, patience, and perseverance. There are no short cuts.

In August, 2009, I was working in a bakery in South Phoenix, Arizona. I literally had my bar card in my pocket, and I was loading bread trucks in the middle of the night for eight dollars an hour. I would start my shift at two in the morning and finish sometime in the afternoon. I was so tired when I woke up; I once wore two different shoes to work. Most of my co-workers were either recent immigrants or had not finished high school. I was working in the bakery, as it was truly the only job I could find. I had graduated law school, passed the bar, and could not find a job as an attorney. As some of you remember, 2009 was in the middle of what many described as The Great Recession, and unemployment rates were the highest they had been since the 1980s.

Here I was, loading bread trucks in the dead of summer in Phoenix, sweating through my shirt and thinking, "I am a licensed lawyer, why am I working at a bakery?" While studying for the Bar, and afterward, I applied for many legal jobs. At first I was picky; later I applied anywhere I could. The one place I really wanted to work was the Public Defender's Office.

I applied at the Maricopa County Public Defender's Office and was interviewed, but was not offered a position. I thought that since I had interned at the Ann Arbor Michigan Public Defender's Office, I would likely get hired. Turned out, I was wrong. I had been optimistic about the Public Defender's Office hiring me. I had great letters from judges in Michigan and great letters of recommendation from my bosses in the Michigan Public Defender's Office. None of the letters helped. I had sent out resumes and cover letters to every legal job I could find. I soon lost track of how many resumes I had mailed. I did not receive even one response thanking me for applying.

I contacted every Cooley Law School alumni that I could find in the Phoenix area. I remember I had a spreadsheet of alumnus that I had gotten from Cooley. I went down the list and contacted every single one. I felt like a telemarketer cold-calling people. Many ignored my phone calls and emails. A few met with me and were helpful and gracious with their time, but no one offered me a job. No one even knew anyone that was hiring. At that time, attorneys that had jobs were thankful to still be employed. One of the alumni that I would later become good friends with told me that he had a pile of over 300 rejection letters when he was looking for work. I knew I was going to be fighting an uphill battle, but I don't think I had figured how steep the hill would be. Most law firms were downsizing and laying off attorneys, and here I was trying to land my first legal job.

After I could not find a legal job, I began looking for non-legal jobs. At first I was kind of picky about the type of job I wanted. I kept telling myself someone *should* give me a good job. I thought, I went through *all this* school, got my masters, and my J.D., passed the bar; all this should be enough, and I *should* get a job. I had been in college and law school nonstop for eight years, and now I was done. I thought attending all of that school would ensure me a job, but, like often before, I was wrong. After a couple of months of not working, I began to look for any kind of job I could find.

I began to apply at every place I could. A low point was an interview at a telemarketing/phone scam place by a person with a cross tattoo on his face. He explained that they did not pay for the first month of work but after that the earning potential was limitless. I applied to be a bike taxi driver and a regular taxi driver. I actually got an interview to sell carpet. I remember how excited I was to get an interview for a minimum wage job because at least they were giving me an interview. Another low point was interviewing at a truck driving school. My interview was in a trailer. The interviewer asked me why I was applying there since I was an attorney. I told him I simply needed a job. I also lied and said I didn't want to be an attorney. I figured it would help my chances of getting hired. It didn't.

Eventually, I learned about an opening at a bakery. The reason I knew of the opening and ultimately got the job was because my friend knew someone that worked there. At orientation I remember the other new hires being very excited because they would be making more than minimum wage. At this point, I was so bummed out from not being able to get a job that I was just happy to be working. I got the job, and I was officially employed as bread truck loader.

I deeply hated working at the bakery, and continued to send out as many legal resumes as I could. I remember checking various websites all the time in the hopes that a new attorney position would be posted. I posted so many profiles on job websites I often lost track of where I already had a profile and what my password was. While working at the bakery, I began to plan opening my own law practice. I had entertained the idea for a long time and had done a lot of planning. I was also fortunate to have had a Law Office Management class in law school.

Over the next several months, the idea of opening my own practice became even more attractive. The more I grew to hate the bakery, the more I wanted my own practice. Almost every experienced attorney I spoke to told me that it could not be done and that I had to work for someone else first. One of the reasons I wanted to write this book is because I could not find anything similar when I needed it. I also wanted to tell young attorneys that opening your own practice right out of law school is possible. Incredibly difficult, but possible. When I was researching starting my own practice, I looked at a lot of law office management books. I could not find a book called "You Work in a Bakery but You Want to Have Your Own Practice; Here Is What to Do," but that was what I needed. I hope this book will serve as a road map for people who find themselves in a similar position.

After a couple of months at the bakery, management learned that I was an attorney. I was approached and told that they wanted me to stay with the bakery and work my way up the corporate ladder. This was good news. I could literally crawl out from the inside of a bread truck. But, there would be a down side. I would be giving up on a law career for the foreseeable future. I had a choice to make. I could play it safe and stay at the bakery, or I could open my own law practice. Open a practice in a city where I had zero connections, zero contacts, zero legal experience, zero clients, and zero savings. I quit the bakery on a Friday and started my own practice the following Monday.

Starting my own practice was not as scary for me as it may have been for other people for one simple reason. The simple reason is that the odds of me becoming a lawyer in the first place were long, at best. The first time I took the LSAT, I received the lowest score of anyone I had ever met. Today, I joke that I still have the lowest score of any attorney I know. I talk about it like a golf score. "You think yours was low? Ha; let me tell you mine." When I received my score I was shocked. I thought I had done everything right to prep for the test. I had studied and taken a prep class; I took the test seriously. How did this happen? I remember getting the results right before going on a family vacation. I was so bummed out that the results pretty much ruined that vacation. I also remember thinking that with my score I would never get into law school.

I retook the LSAT and did a little bit better, so I applied to a bunch of different schools that all promptly rejected me. Not one school even waitlisted me. I had been the kid who watched every *Law and Order* episode and told everyone who would listen that I wanted to be a lawyer. In high school, I was voted "Most Likely to Become a Lawyer." I had wanted to be a lawyer for as long as I could remember. Now I had to deal with the reality that I would not become a lawyer. When I had pretty much given up on the idea of law school, I was presented an opportunity.

I remember getting a flier from Thomas M. Cooley School of Law and thinking, is this a real law school? I had never heard of the place. I knew that the school was in Michigan and I knew nothing about Michigan. Not only had I never been to Michigan, but I had never been to the Midwest. I applied because it was my last chance to go to law school, and it was an opportunity to pursue a dream that I had had for as long as I could remember. One of the recurring themes of this book is taking advantage of opportunities when they present themselves. Cooley had given me an opportunity.

Cooley accepted me and I was off to Michigan. I moved to Lansing in the dead of winter. I did not know anyone, and it was two days before New Years' Eve. I remember standing on the balcony of my studio apartment in the snow facing the old Oldsmobile plant and thinking this was an ominous sign. For the next three years, I would struggle with grades like I never imagined I could. Before this, school had always been fairly easy for me. I had good grades in high school, good grades in undergrad, and very good grades in grad school. I was always able to do well without working very hard. Now I was studying a ton and having a hard time passing classes. I had heard, like every law student, the old saying that the first year they scare you to death, the second year they work you to death, and the third year they bore you to death. For three years, I felt like I was being worked to death. I got one A in law school. It was a one credit independent study class my last term of my last year. That nicely summarizes my academic life in law school.

I was nearly done with law school and now I had THE BAR EXAM to look forward to. At Cooley I took a bar prep course, and they showed us a graph. In the graph, you put in your law school GPA and your LSAT score and it gave you your estimated percentage of passing the bar. I suppose this graph was based on past bar takers. When I plotted my info, the graph told me I had a seventeen percent chance of passing. This meant I had a seventy-three percent chance of failing.

As I spent the next several months studying, I kept thinking about the seventeen percent. In a way, knowing about the seventeen percent was a negative because it scared me and put doubt in my head. But, it also helped. It helped because it motivated me to study harder. Like the old cliché about how no one believes in you. One of the recurring themes of this book is turning negatives into positives. I tried to turn the seventeen percent into a positive.

I took studying seriously and tried to take everyone's advice. Anyone that has ever taken the bar loves to give advice. Some of the advice is not great. Some was just plain terrible. One person told me not to study. Some of the best advice that I received is to treat studying as a full time job. This approach is nothing new, but very valuable nonetheless. Be at your desk on time in the morning and study all day with short breaks. I know for some people, studying full time is not an option, and I understand that.

You have to make time for studying or you are likely to fail. There are few super-geniuses that can pass without studying. I knew I was not one of those people. My wife, then my girlfriend, was also studying for the bar, so she understood what I was going through. Having someone to study with was helpful. Even though we never actually studied together, I liked knowing that I was not going through everything on my own. Long, tedious, and painful story made short—I passed the Bar. I had passed by approximately one multiple-choice question, but I passed. I had passed the Bar and could not find a job. This brings us back to the bakery.

WHY THIS BOOK IS HELPFUL AND DIFFERENT

Lawyers love giving advice. The lawyers that love to give advice more than any other kind of lawyer are the ones that write books telling other new attorneys what to do. Although my goal is the same as anyone that has ever written this type of book—to help new or young attorneys build their own practice and to be professional and ethical in the process —my approach is different.

There are a lot of law office management and practice building books on the market. Many tell you that there is a secret or a system or tricks to building a practice. Some promise sure-fire methods for success. Yet other books feel like an infomercial, which is never good. Authors from Ivy League schools write many law office management books. Authors with very impressive resumes that are as long as a short story write many law office management books. In fact, many of the books are quite good. Many of the books were of great use when I was starting my own practice. My goal here is not to criticize other books. My goal is quite different.

My goal is to offer a book that I wish had been around when I was starting my own practice: a book written by a young lawyer, for young lawyers and law students. A book that is useful, insightful, entertaining, down to earth, and written by someone that not only started their own practice from nothing, but also did not go to a top tier law school. I went to a law school that is far from an Ivy League law school. Whether I accomplish these goals or not will be for you to decide. Some of my opinions will differ from those of other attorneys. Remember, often there is more than one correct approach. Two attorneys can do the same thing in two different ways and both do it correctly.

I will explain my reasoning as I go, and I hope my explanations will be useful to you when it comes time to make these decisions. This book is simple by design. My goal was to write a concise, straightforward text. I have also tried to be honest about the good and the bad in the legal profession. Too many books paint a rosy picture, which is a disservice to young attorneys. I think young attorneys should know not only the benefits of having their own practice, but the drawbacks as well. There is one last reason this book is different. Many law office management books only give the opinion of the author. I have tried to include approaches and philosophies from a number of excellent attorneys and to combine them in one place. While doing the research for this book, I went to excellent attorneys and asked them their opinions on what new attorneys should know coming into practice. I also asked them what they wish they would have known about the legal profession and running their own office that they know now but didn't know when starting out. I think many of their answers will be valuable to new attorneys. I also spoke to many judges and asked them what they wish young attorneys knew and what they should do when they are starting out. So now I have told you why this book is different. The question you should now be asking is, "Why should we listen to you?"

CHAPTER 2
WHY SHOULD I LISTEN TO THIS GUY? DOES HE KNOW WHAT HE'S TALKING ABOUT?

Out of necessity, I had to build a law practice from nothing. I didn't set out to build a practice from scratch just to see if I could. I didn't have a choice. I had bills to pay. I also liked to eat and needed money to pay for food. I was tired of the bakery, and I was tired of not getting my phone calls returned from law firms. Looking back, it was amazing how little I knew. In hindsight, not knowing much was a blessing, because I didn't know everything I had ahead of me and what huge challenges I had yet to face.

When I started, I had zero management experience. I had no knowledge of business, managing a business, growing a business, establishing a business, or what it meant to be a business owner. I knew nothing about business. I had never even been an assistant manager at a McDonalds like many of my friends had been. I had read books and articles, but the difference between reading about owning a business and actually running a business is analogous to reading about being chased by a bear as opposed to actually being chased by a bear. One is scarier than the other.

My lack of business experience was one problem, but it was not my biggest problem. My biggest problem was that I had no real-world legal experience. I say real-world experience because real-world law experience is very different than law school law experience. I had never worked at a firm or an agency. I had volunteered at two firms and interned at the public defender's office, but I had never had an actual legal job. I never second chaired a trial, never filed a motion, had an office, or prepped a case for trial. I had never met with a client without a supervising attorney present. Not only did I not have any legal work experience, but I knew nothing about the local legal market.

Building a practice while not knowing anything about business was only half of my problem. Not only was I clueless about how to run a business, I also had no connections to attorneys or judges in the Phoenix area. I didn't have any local attorneys that I could call and ask for help. I had family-friend attorneys in Portland, Oregon, and they could help with general questions, but they could do little for local questions. Needless to say, I would be figuring out a lot on my own. Again, the point is not to talk about how I figured out everything out on my own. The point is that I did learn a lot on my own that I hope to pass to others.

THERE IS NO SUBSTITUTE FOR EXPERIENCE

The best response I have to our question, "Why Listen to Me?" is that I can offer you experience. In the past four years I have been inside a courtroom practically every single day. Not only have I been in court almost every day, I have also spent a lot of weekends in jail court and in the office. The courts I have practiced in have varied a lot. Some of the courthouses were in Superior Courts, many were in different city courts, some were in Justice of Peace Courts, and some were simply hearing courtrooms. In the past month alone I have appeared in numerous superior courtrooms, two justice courts, and seven different municipal courts.

I have dealt with every kind of client, prosecutor, judge, and court staff personality imaginable. I like to think that I learned something from all of them along the way. In those courtrooms I have appeared in front of close to one hundred judges and countless prosecutors. In 2012 alone, I represented 4500 in-custody defendants. This is not counting out of custody defendants or private clients. I have had numerous non-jury trials and dozens of jury trials. I have handled criminal cases spanning from armed robbery to photo radar tickets and everything in between.

Another way I learned a lot was from covering other attorneys. Covering is when an attorney pays you to go to court in his place. There are a million reasons why an attorney may need coverage. He may be sick, he may not want to go to court, he may have a scheduling conflict, or he could be on vacation. I will speak more at length about coverage later on. I have covered for over one hundred attorneys and learned a lot from them. Some were excellent, some were terrible, and many are in-between.

I have made a lot of mistakes along the way and tried to learn from all of them. Some of my mistakes were really little and some were not so little. All attorneys make mistakes, and I have probably made more than many. I was learning as I went. Often, no one was available to teach me when I was doing something wrong. A lot of the time, I would jump into cases that were over my head. Kind of like the story of the person who jumps over a ravine and, half way over, looks down and sees a giant tiger. An important lesson throughout this book is that all attorneys make mistakes. The difference between the good ones and the bad ones is, in part, if they learn from their mistakes. I see a lot of bad attorneys make the same mistake over and over and never move on.

One last reason I can offer advice is that I have tried to learn from other solo lawyers' mistakes. I have seen more than a couple lawyers fail and I have tried to not repeat their mistakes. I have always felt that learning from other people's mistakes is a lot easier than learning from your own. Many of the mistakes I saw are covered in this book and are easy to avoid if you are careful. New solo practices fail for many of the same reasons that any new business can fail. I will point out many of the pitfalls that new attorneys should watch out for.

CHAPTER 3
A FEW WORDS ON SUCCEEDING IN THE LEGAL PROFESSION

Succeeding at running your own practice or establishing a good reputation in the legal profession is no different than succeeding in any field. Some attorneys will tell you how being an attorney is *so* different than any other profession. They are right in some ways, but wrong in one big way. The basic principles of success are the same for any profession. Working on achieving excellence is the same no matter if you are a plumber, lawyer, or brain surgeon. The basic principles are simple. They are principles that you don't need to read in a book to understand. If you asked a sixth grader what it takes to succeed in business, many of them would give you the correct answer. Much of this book is about succeeding in the legal profession and at running your own practice, but the basic principles of success are simple. Work hard (ideally, work harder than everyone else), treat people well, be honest, and be patient. The ideas are simple. Like most things, however, the difficulty is in the execution.

Saying that you should work hard is simple. Everyone says they want to work hard, but many people don't actually want to. Many new attorneys don't want to work weekends, evenings, and holidays. In 2011 and 2012, I worked jail court every major holiday weekend. When I was talking to an attorney who is not known for his work ethic, the subject of me working weekends came up. The other attorney said that he thought it was crappy that I had to work major holidays and that he would not work holidays. I told him that it was not a matter of wanting to work holidays, but a matter of wanting to grow my practice and to make more money . . . so I worked those holidays. A person has to be driven and hard working to succeed.

Since I started teaching, I have always extended the same invitation to all my students and all the groups I have spoken to. I always invite everyone to come to court to shadow me around. If someone wants to watch a trial, a pretrial, or a hearing, they are always welcome to come. Over the past year I have extended this offer to approximately 300 students. Out of those 300, about 40 expressed interest in coming to court. Out of those 40, about 10 actually came to court once. Out of those 10, 1 student has come to court with me regularly. She continues to ask me to go to court whenever she can and helps in any way she can. She goes to court without me paying her. She goes to court with me to have the opportunity to learn. Out of all the students I have invited to go to court, guess which student I think will succeed?

No book can teach work ethic and determination. A person is either driven to work hard and succeed or he's not. If a person is driven, he will generally succeed in whatever he is doing. Being driven is more important than being smart. We have all known smart people that were not driven. When I am looking for an attorney or an intern, I will take driven over smart any day. I can teach a person to practice. I cannot teach a person drive and hard work.

YOU ARE RESPONSIBLE FOR YOUR OWN SUCCESS

Another important lesson on succeeding in the legal profession may seem harsh, but I believe it to be true. No one cares if you succeed or fail. It is your responsibility to succeed. In other words, no one is owed success. This does not mean that you will not have people around that will be helping you, rooting for you, and wanting you to succeed. Obviously, you will have family members, mentors, loved ones, and colleagues that will root for your success. But, ultimately, no one besides you can make you succeed or fail.

I believe it is very important to think actively about the principle that success or failure is dependent on you. If a person begins his career making excuses, those excuses can consume him. When I graduated law school, the unemployment rate was the highest since the 1980s. On top of the bad economy, I had every other challenge facing me that I have already spoken about.

If I had started my practice thinking about how bad the economy was and thinking that if I fail it will be the economy's fault and not my own, this thought process would have only hurt and not helped me. Always remember that you are responsible for the things you can control, like your reputation and how your peers and clients view you in the legal community.

I see how a negative outlook affects people every day, through my clients and other attorneys. Almost every day I hear from my clients how everything is someone else's fault. Nothing is ever his or her own fault or his or her responsibility. Every day I hear from clients that they can't find a job because the economy is bad, or they can't find a job because the job they want is hard to get, etc. I often think about how these people's lives would be better if they had a different outlook and attitude. Instead of saying "the economy is bad and I can't find a job," some people thought "even though the economy is bad, I will not give up until I find a job, and it's my responsibility to find a job." The job thing is just one example, but you get the idea.

Too often, I hear fellow lawyers make excuses why their practice is not doing well or they are not making enough money. Rarely do they examine their attitude and outlook. If these attorneys focused on the positive and not the negative, they would be much happier. This is not to say you should not take outside factors into account. You must have the attitude that you will determine your own future. Obviously, you should think about outside forces like the current economy, but do not let the outside forces determine your outlook and your goals. Another factor that will help to determine if you succeed or fail is how perseverant you are.

As a new attorney, it is important for you to remember that often things will not work the first time you try them. An argument that you may think is great may get shot down at trial. A position that you feel you are qualified for may be given to someone else. You must remember to keep trying and trying and trying. I have a friend who wanted to be a patent attorney. To be a patent attorney you have to take a separate huge exam called The Patent Bar. My friend studied really hard and took the test and failed. He took it again and failed. He took the exam a third and fourth time and failed each time. He did not give up and continued to study and took the exam a fifth time. My friend passed and is now an incredibly successful patent attorney.

BE CAREFUL WHO YOU TAKE ADVICE FROM

When you are starting out either as a new lawyer working for someone else or as a new lawyer starting your own practice, every lawyer you meet will try to give you advice. Be careful from whom you take advice. For example, if a lawyer is giving you advice on how to do jury trials but he has not done a jury trial himself in ten years, this should be a red flag. It is important to remember that bad advice is often worse than no advice. As a new lawyer, you will have the problem of often not knowing good advice from bad advice. You must use your own judgment and intuition. The good news is that often the bad advice is so bad it will be easy to spot.

Another common example of lawyers giving new attorneys advice is how to succeed and make lots of money. When I was starting out, a lot of attorneys told me how to build a large, successful practice. The problem was that the lawyers had practices that were barely afloat. I have seen these attorneys who tell me how well they have done for themselves walk out to cars that barely start. My intent is not to imply that young attorneys should not take advice from other attorneys, but be careful to who you listen to.

One good piece of advice, and one that I still use today, is to ask other attorneys if the person giving you advice knows what they are talking about. When I was starting out, I got a lot of trial advice from other attorneys. I would almost always run their advice by one of my mentors to see what they would say. Sometimes they would say it was great advice and that it made sense, so I would listen to that advice. On more than one occasion, they told me it was terrible advice and would explain why it was terrible advice and I would know not to listen to it. Again, when you are new you will not know a lot about the law, but always listen to your own intuition. If something doesn't sound right, always listen to your gut.

BE WILLING TO WORK FOR FREE

"You have to pay the cost to be the boss" *–Biggie Smalls-*

When starting out, you must be willing to work for free. There are a couple of reasons why. The first is to get experience. There is no substitute for experience in the legal profession or any profession. One of the best ways to get experience is by offering to work for free. While in law school, I volunteered for two different law offices and learned a lot from both of them. One of the attorneys was a former prosecutor who taught me a lot about criminal defense. The other lawyer I volunteered for did a little bit of everything, but did not do anything well. I learned a lot of what *not* to do from him. I learned how not to treat your staff or your clients and other valuable lessons. It is very important to remember that you must gain experience any way you can. If someone is willing to pay you to learn that's great, but often not very realistic.

The other reason you must be willing to work for free is to show other attorneys that you are serious about building your practice and your career. Even in large markets, the legal community is usually pretty small. In general, bankruptcy attorneys know most other bankruptcy attorneys and criminal defense attorneys know other criminal defense attorneys, etc. The point is that attorneys talk about who the good attorneys are and who the bad attorneys are. By being willing to work for free, you show other attorneys that you are serious about learning your craft and gaining experience. When you talk to most successful attorneys, they will tell you they did more than a little bit of free work for other attorneys when they were starting out.

When I was starting out I did quite a bit of free legal research for other attorneys. Even though I was not getting paid for the work, I was showing those attorneys that I was serious about learning. Today, I have working relationships with many of those attorneys. I also made a lot of court appearances for other attorneys at no charge. One way to look at it is that I was doing free work. I looked at it differently. I looked at it as building relationships and gaining valuable experience. If an attorney or an agency that you respect asks you to help out for free and you say no, they will remember.

Building relationships is more valuable than making a quick buck. When I started my own practice, I really wanted to get a contract with the City of Phoenix Public Defender's Office. The City of Phoenix does not have full time public defenders but pays private attorneys to handle indigent clients and their criminal matters. The contracts are very coveted, and there are many more applicants every year than there are contracts to be awarded. Almost everyone that has a contract originally started at the county public defender's office or one of the prosecutor agencies, either city or county. I had never worked for an agency so I knew I had to prove myself to get a contract. I think that one of the factors that led me to being awarded a contract so quickly was my willingness to work for the office for free.

Whenever the office called me and asked me if I could fill in, I was always there. Sometimes they could pay me and other times they could not. I never complained and always showed up. Just today as I was writing, the office asked me to fill in. Another attorney was running late as he got stuck in Superior Court. I volunteered to help, because not only is it the right thing to do, it is good for business.

This is just one of many examples that I have had where I was willing to work for free where it benefited my career down the road. The "down the road" part is important. Rarely are there instant payoffs. Also, remember that when you are starting out, you will have plenty of free time on your hands, so it is beneficial to simply help out. In the beginning, you will have the choice of working for free and learning or sitting at home and waiting for the phone to ring.

NETWORKING AND MENTORS

I don't like the word "networking," but it is an important word. When you are new, you do not have a lot of connections. The way you get access to opportunities is through who you know. As I have mentioned, many of the best positions, contracts, and opportunities are not advertised. You need to have connections to learn about opportunities. The way you make connections is through networking. Networking does not have to be formal. You don't have to be in a large room with a bunch of people with nametags where everyone introduces himself or herself and shares their favorite color.

In all areas, there are events that young attorneys should be attending regularly. There will be State Bar conferences and meetings. There will be events for young attorneys and for attorneys in different areas of law. There are events for female attorneys and for minority groups. In Arizona, there are monthly young lawyer events held at restaurants or bars. I always tell my students to go to these events because you never know who you will meet and what opportunity will be presented to you. I once got a good private client by referral from an attorney I met at a bank get together.

Many of the best networking opportunities are informal. If you have an opportunity to meet someone, you should do it. When I was new, I would always introduce myself to other attorneys. I would tell them that I was new and often strike up a conversation. Some of these conversations resulted in coverage jobs for me. Sometimes the attorneys themselves didn't need coverage but they knew someone who did. More than once I've received a phone call from an attorney telling me they heard about me from another attorney.

If there is an attorney you want to learn from, invite them to lunch or coffee. Some will say no, and you have lost nothing. I have invited many attorneys to lunch or to coffee that have not responded. Some of the best connections I have made, however, were from inviting other attorneys to coffee or lunch. Whether you are in a firm or on your own, you will need a mentor or mentors.

Having a good mentor can have a huge impact on your career. Not only can a good mentor enhance your career, the relationship can determine whether your practice succeeds or fails. If you are at a firm, finding a mentor should not be very difficult; there will be people at the firm. If the firm is large, you will have a supervising attorney or someone actually assigned to you as a mentor. If you are on your own, it will be up to you to find a mentor.

I have had many mentors, but there is one to whom I owe the most. I met him at a young-lawyer event. I introduced myself and invited him to lunch. After lunch, I asked him if I could go to court with him to learn. I started going to court with him and I went often. I would call him almost every evening and see what he had on his schedule the following day. I spent several months following him around and learning a ton. Following him around had two benefits. I was learning from him, but he was also introducing me to people. He would say that I was new and if anyone needed coverage to call me. All my first coverage clients came about from this experience. If it were not for him, I am not sure if my practice would have survived. I was lucky and fortunate to find a great mentor.

Like with everything, luck favors the motivated. If I had not asked to come to court and taken it upon myself to come, nothing good would have resulted from the meeting. Always remember that you need the mentor much more than they need you. When offering your services to someone, it is on you to convince the person why they should let you help them. Be willing to do free legal research or free coverage. Make sure the attorney you want to work with knows that you are willing to help. You must be willing to prove yourself.

There is an *Entourage* episode where an assistant is trying to get promoted to an agent. The assistant's boss makes him sit outside the house until the middle of the night. The reason the assistant has to sit outside for half the night is to show the boss that he is committed and willing to do anything to get the promotion. Young attorneys must also be willing to do anything to show their mentors that they are serious. My mentor knew that he could call me at any time and I would make myself available to help in any way that I could.

I have had many people say they wanted to come to court with me only to blow me off at the last minute. I have had people not show up at all. As soon as someone has not shown up for court and not taken the time to text me or email me, there is zero chance that I will invite them to shadow me again. Most attorneys want to be helpful to young attorneys, but no one likes having their time wasted. You must demonstrate that you are serious. One of the ways you demonstrate you are serious is by contacting a prospective mentor more than once.

I have a good attorney friend that I met because he was a Cooley alumnus. I found him on the alumni database and we exchanged a couple of emails before I moved to Arizona from Michigan. When we met for lunch once I moved, he told me something that really stuck with me. He told me that he had a lot of Cooley grads reach out to him and want to meet him. He told me that they had to reach out to him more than once. He told me if someone reached out to him once, or had lunch with him once he didn't really remember them and wouldn't do a lot for them. I now have students and alumni reaching out to me and I do the same thing. I want to know someone is committed and devoted to succeeding before I go out of my way to help them. Why would I help someone who is not serious about helping himself?

CHAPTER 4
THE LEGAL PROFESSION
IS CHANGING

This should not come as a shock to anyone. Entire books have been written on how the profession is changing. Everything from how law schools teach students to how firms are run is in a state of flux. My goal for this chapter is to quickly point out several ways the profession is changing and why. One of the biggest changes is that there are more lawyers and fewer jobs. More and more people are going to law school, while at the same time, the bad economy and other factors are affecting the legal job market. A simple supply and demand analysis shows us that there is a higher supply of lawyers than a demand for them.

What this means for new attorneys is that they must be more creative, flexible, and willing to adapt to survive. One of my biggest goals for this book is to get law students and recent law school graduates to start thinking outside the box (pardon the cliché). New attorneys must evolve past the old ways of doing things. Like all species, attorneys must evolve. Young attorneys must be creative in how they run their practices and how they grow their practices.

For better or worse, the old-school model of graduating law school, easily finding a job, and staying with one firm your entire career is generally not realistic anymore. New lawyers must evolve to survive. Think of the dinosaurs who, unfortunately, are not with us anymore. There are still some attorneys who graduate and easily find work, but this is becoming the exception. I am a big believer in hoping for the best but preparing for the worst. If you graduate and easily find a great job, that is great, but what if you don't, then what?

How people receive legal services is also changing. There are more document preparation services, paralegals, and websites that are taking work away from attorneys. Most of us have seen the billboards or newspaper ads saying "DIVORCE FOR $200" or something similar. If you are looking to get a divorce you have several options. You can go to a traditional divorce/family law lawyer who tells you they can do your divorce for several thousand dollars. Or, you can have a document prep place do your divorce for $200. As a consumer, the $200 place is tempting.

Part of the reason that the document preparation place is tempting is because people, usually wrongly, believe they can solve their own legal problems and don't need the services of an attorney. Even though no one would ever attempt to do their own surgery to save money by not paying a surgeon, people will try to handle their own legal matter to save money on paying a lawyer. Online legal service providers have also cut into how much work lawyers have.

Much like the $200 divorce, many of us have seen ads for web services that tell you that you don't need to pay a high priced attorney and can do everything on your own with their help for a fraction of the price. Between do-it-yourself law books, document prep places, and online legal services, it is becoming harder and harder for attorneys to get clients.

Although how people get legal services is changing, law firms themselves are also changing. Today, it is hard to go a week without seeing a story about some mega firm filing for bankruptcy or dissolving and leaving everyone out of work. There was a time that once you got hired at a big prestigious firm, you had job security for life. That time is largely gone. In 2012, one of the largest law firms in the world with over 1300 partners filed for bankruptcy.[1] Can you imagine being one of the

---

[1] http://www.forbes.com/sites/danielfisher/2012/05/29/dewey-leboeuf- bankruptcy-a-one-off-but-still/

1300 hundred attorneys? You worked hard, got a job at a great firm, and thought you would be at that firm for a long time. Then, one perfectly good day, you get an email or a phone call that the firm is closing and that you are out of work.

Unfortunately for young attorneys, huge firm closings are not as rare as one would think or hope. The reasons large firms go out of business are beyond the scope of this book, but the point is that there is less job security in large firms than there used to be, and young or new lawyers must be prepared for this. Again, hope for the best, but prepare for the worst.

There are not only fewer "big law" jobs than in the past, but there are more and more attorneys starting their own practices. Attorneys that in the past would have been at a firm or a government agency may have to start their own practice, as they have no choice. What this means is that there are more attorneys competing over the same clients. So where in the past there might have been 10 lawyers competing over 100 clients, now there are 100 lawyers competing over those same 100 clients.

A fun exercise is to Google your hometown and the type of law that you are interested in. For example, Google "Phoenix and Business Lawyer." You will be amazed by how many lawyers there are all competing over the same clients. I practice criminal law exclusively in the Phoenix area and it seems like every day I meet another attorney that is hanging his or her own shingle and hoping to practice criminal law. There is no reason to think that more and more attorneys competing over the same clients is likely to change anytime soon.

Another change that is happening is how people perceive lawyers. I would equate the change with how people viewed politicians versus how politicians are viewed today. From what I understand, when someone used to aspire to be a politician, it was considered a noble calling and was respected by the public. Today if someone says they are a politician, thoughts of corruptions, selfishness, and not getting anything done probably come to mind. Lawyers face a similar problem. In general, lawyers are not viewed as problem solvers and helpers. There are several reasons for the change.

I think one of the big reasons for the negative way lawyers are viewed is that many people don't understand what lawyers actually do. I deal with a lot of people that don't understand what it is I do as a criminal defense attorney. I often have people ask me how I feel about getting guilty people out of prison and out from responsibility for their actions.

Almost every defense attorney has, at one point or another, been asked how they can do what they do. The not-so-subtle implication being that our work is so horrible that a normal person would never want to do it. Many of us heard the horrible phrase that a lawyer "got someone off on a technicality." That technicality is the Constitution of the United States, but I digress.

Part of the problem is that most non-lawyers blame lawyers for the actions of the lawyer's clients. But when a criminal defense attorney represents someone charged with some horrible crime, it obviously doesn't mean that that lawyer endorses the actions of his client. The same principle is true in civil cases. When a client asks a lawyer to help with a cause that is important to the client but not to the lawyer, it does not mean that the lawyer is endorsing that issue.

One example that comes to mind is when ACLU was defending the North American Man Boy Love Association. What the ACLU was defending was the First Amendment and not what NAMBLA stood for, but many people blamed the lawyers of the ACLU for representing such a despicable group. Fighting for the First Amendment and other worthy causes often means that lawyers have to represent unpopular causes as a way to defend liberties that everyone values.

How the media portrays lawyers hasn't helped either. In almost any movie or TV show where there is an attorney, the chances are that the attorney is portrayed as unethical or underhanded or not trustworthy. Most lawyers in movies or TV shows are somewhere between shifty and evil. Modern shows such as *The Sopranos*, *The Wire*, and *Breaking Bad* all have attorneys that lie, do unethical things, and are portrayed in a bad light.

Breaking Bad features an attorney that is not only unethical but is actively involved in helping his clients commit crime. The attorney not only constantly lies but also often goes behind his client's back to reveal confidential information. When I teach Professional Responsibility, I often play clips of the show and tell my students to do the opposite of what the attorney does to comply with the Model Ethical Rules. Even though most people watching the show know to some extent that the character is a comedic fictional character, I think many people watching think the character is just an exaggerated version of what real defense lawyers are like.

While thinking about this chapter, I tried to think of popular movies or TV shows that depict attorneys in a positive light. I was trying to think of examples where lawyers are ethical and do the right thing, but I could not come up with many examples. All this goes to show that new or young attorneys must work that much harder to show that real attorneys are ethical and honest so that attorneys can begin to work towards restoring a positive image. Young and new attorneys must remember that they represent an entire profession whether they want to or not. Every time one lawyer is dishonest or unethical it reflects poorly on the entire profession. New and young attorneys must never forget this.

The last major reason for why attorneys are viewed as unethical is what the public perceives as "frivolous lawsuits." Chances are that when an attorney tells someone what they do, one of the first questions they will get asked about are "frivolous lawsuits" and how attorneys are allowed to represent people in these cases. One of the most famous cases that attorneys are commonly asked about is the McDonald's hot coffee case. Many of you know about this case, but for those that don't, it involved a woman spilling hot coffee on her lap and suing the restaurant for the coffee being too hot.[2] The jury found for the woman and gave her $200,000 in actual damages. The reason the case made news was because the jury also awarded 2.7 million dollars to the plaintiff. There was a lot of national coverage of the story and people were outraged that someone would get so much money for spilling coffee on herself. There was a lot of

---

[2] http://www.lectlaw.com/files/cur78.htm

information that people did not know about the case, which would probably change their views. According to reports:

> The sweatpants Liebeck was wearing absorbed the coffee and held it next to her skin. A vascular surgeon determined that Liebeck suffered full thickness burns (or third-degree burns) over 6 percent of her body, including her inner thighs, perineum, buttocks, and genital and groin areas. She was hospitalized for eight days, during which time she underwent skin grafting. Liebeck, who also underwent debridement treatments, sought to settle her claim for $20,000, but McDonalds refused.[3]

Most people did not know that there had been hundreds of complaints against McDonalds for their coffee being too hot. Many people did not know that McDonalds had a policy of keeping their coffee very hot, had discussed the issue, and chosen to not address the problem.[4] Lastly, 2.7 million dollars sounds like a lot of money, but it is the amount that McDonalds makes off coffee in two days. The amount of punitive damages was later reduced to $480,000 dollars by the court.[5] The point is that many people think of attorneys as taking on these "frivolous" lawsuits even though they are often serious.

---

[3] http://www.lectlaw.com/files/cur78.htm
[4] http://www.lectlaw.com/files/cur78.htm
[5] http://www.lectlaw.com/files/cur78.htm

CHAPTER 5
SHOULD YOU START YOUR OWN PRACTICE?

Having your own practice can be the best thing in the world. For me, the advantages far outweigh the disadvantages. There are many advantages and some disadvantages, and I'll talk about them in more detail in a bit. Having your own practice is not for everyone. This is incredibly important and worth repeating. Having your own practice is *not* for everyone. The logical question is, who should and who should not have their own practice? First, who should not start their own practice?

When you are deciding on whether or not you should start your own practice, you *must* be honest with yourself. If you are not self-motivated, you should not have your own practice. If you are averse to all risk, you should not have your own practice. There is obvious risk in starting your own practice. The practice could fail. If do not address this reality, you are not being honest with yourself.

If you prefer just getting a paycheck for your work and do not want all the responsibility on you, you should not have your own practice. If you are painfully shy and want to avoid client interaction, you should not start your own practice. It is worth mentioning that there are plenty of excellent lawyers that have no interest in having their own practice and there is nothing wrong with this. Some attorneys do not want the headache of dealing with running the business; some have found great bosses and do not want to leave, and obviously there is nothing wrong with this. I know many excellent attorneys that have chosen to spend their entire careers at a government agency. Some attorneys are perfectly happy not having their own practice and not being in the private sector. Again, the key is that you have to be honest with yourself and what you want.

That being said, you may not know what you want right away and this is okay, too. I meet a lot of students who, for example, say they want to be prosecutors until they spend a day with me or a different defense attorney in court and suddenly they don't want to be prosecutors anymore. Some people think they want to have their own practice until they realize all the planning, managing, and organizing that go into it, and then they want to work for someone else.

I have developed a simple test for deciding if you should have your own practice. Ask yourself if you are willing to outwork everyone. If the answer is yes, you should think about having your own practice. If the answer is no, you should not have your own practice. If you are willing to wake up earlier, stay at work longer, and out-hustle other attorneys, you should think about having your own practice. If you decide to have your own practice, the next factor to think about is timing.

TIMING

One of the hardest decisions facing attorneys is when to start their own practice. Should they do it right away, wait a couple of years, or wait more than a couple of years? Obviously, there are different opinions and philosophies. A common and traditional view is that it is a good idea to work for someone else for a couple of years and then start your own practice. There are advantages to this model but also several hidden risks. The major advantage is that someone takes you under his wing and teaches you the ropes. Someone teaches you how to prepare documents and motions, how to go to court, and how to handle clients and their problems. Like a good mentor, they slowly bring you up and you learn as you go while earning a living. This is all great sounding, but there are several hidden risks that many, if not all, new attorneys do not think about.

Say, for example, you get a job at a firm or an agency and the place is terrible. Every term, I see my law students take jobs with firms that I know are disreputable, dishonest, and will teach the students terrible habits. The problem is, that with the students being new attorneys, they do not know that what they are learning is wrong. New attorneys often wrongly assume that just because they are learning they are automatically learning the correct way of doing things. For attorneys, as in any profession, is it very difficult to unlearn bad habits and virtually impossible do undo a bad reputation. This point brings us to the next hidden danger of working for someone else.

If you are a new attorney, you may get a job for a bad firm and you figure it's okay because you are a good attorney and you are honest and your reputation will be good. You figure the place you work at has a less than stellar reputation, but your own personal reputation will not be affected. The problem with this is that whether it is fair or not, an attorney takes on the reputation of the place where he or she works. If you work for a terrible or dishonest firm, other attorneys will associate the bad traits of that firm with you.

I know several very good attorneys at bad firms, and I know the reputation of those attorneys has suffered as a result of where they work. As I have mentioned and will continue to mention, your reputation is the single most important thing you have as an attorney. Unfortunately, there are other hidden dangers when you work for someone else.

Say you have found a great job, your mentor is great, the firm has a great reputation, and you have learned a lot. Two or three years go by and you decide you want to go out on your own. You have about twenty or thirty of your own clients that you have brought to the firm and you figure the clients will go with you to your new solo firm. You come to your boss and say, "Thanks for everything, I am leaving and taking my clients with me." Your boss says, "Great, good luck, but the clients belong to the firm, and if you try taking them we will sue you into non-existence." This actually happened to an attorney friend of mine. When she left one firm and tried to take her clients to her new firm, the old firm sued her, and it has been a huge strain on her.

When I started my practice I had no clients but I always knew that the clients that I got were my own and not the firms' that I was working for. Remember that it's better to have a few clients that are yours then to have many clients of whom zero are yours. This is something to think about, because if you leave a firm and you are not allowed to take any of the firm's clients, how will you make money? This brings us to the last hazard of working for someone else before starting your own practice.

Say you have been working for one or several firms for five or seven or ten years. Things are going well and you are thinking of starting your own practice. You may have one or two kids that you did not have when you finished law school. You have a mortgage and are used to a certain lifestyle. An attorney in this scenario may be used to certain vacations, cars, and other things (think of lawyer stereotypes such as golf club memberships).

Say you are making $100,000 a year. You want to leave your job because maybe you don't like the work, maybe you don't like your bosses or the firm structure, or for whatever reason. The problem is that many attorneys in such scenarios realize that they cannot afford to leave. They realize in many ways that they would be starting over if they went out on their own. Many attorneys get stuck at firms under similar circumstances.

Many attorneys working for government agencies get stuck in a similar problem that has to do with their pensions. "Golden handcuffs" is an expression that most government attorneys are familiar with, and it works like this: A government attorney usually must stay at an agency for a certain number of years before her pension vests. So, first the attorney must stay at an agency for a certain number of years, often five years. Next, attorneys are often worried that if they leave they will not get an actual retirement. Some attorneys end up spending their entire careers at an agency that they might have otherwise left because the pension is so important to them.

For the above reasons, I am an advocate of people starting their own practices sooner rather than later. When I decided to start my own practice, I figured it would take me about three years to establish. I was twenty-seven at the time, and I figured if

I could have a running practice by the time I was thirty, I would be happy. I also figured, and I think most attorneys would agree, that it is easier to fail when you are young than when you are older.

Let's look at our example of the attorney at the firm making $100,000 a year. If my practice had failed, I would have been out a couple thousand dollars, but not much else. If the experienced attorney fails she may lose her house, her cars, and jeopardize her entire lifestyle and the future of her children. The stakes of me failing when I started were so much lower because I had less to lose; I had no money or house, so it took some of the pressure off me when I did start.

I can't tell anyone when the perfect time to start their own practice is, but I can tell you I have never met an attorney that regretted going out on his own. I can also tell you that I have spoken to many attorneys that eventually went out on their own and wish they had done it sooner for many of the reasons above. One attorney comes to mind. He is one of the best criminal defense attorneys in town and spent close to fourteen years working for other attorneys. He told me that he always wanted to go out on his own but had children and was worried. He told me that once he finally did go out on his own he was mad he didn't do it much sooner.

So when is the best time to go out on your own? There is no simple answer. Ideally, you can get some experience working for someone else and then go out on your own. Later on, I will argue that for some people going out on their own right out of law school can be a good idea, but it is not for everyone.

ADVANTAGES AND DISADVANTAGES OF HAVING YOUR OWN PRACTICE

One of the biggest advantages to working for yourself is that you work for yourself. It is hard to describe how nice it is not having a boss. All of us have had bosses, and a good boss can be pleasant to work for. Most of us have also had terrible bosses, and I have had more than my fair share. Even if you are fortunate to have a good boss, you are still answering to someone else. Someone above you is making decisions for you. For some people, this is not a problem, but for me, having the opportunity to work for myself was always very enticing.

There are many benefits that people may not initially think of. For me, being able to go on vacation or to take a day off is priceless. As I am writing this chapter, it is a Thursday and I did not have any court appearances, so I stayed home and did what I wanted to do. I didn't have to check in with my boss and ask if I could stay home. Being able to go on vacation when I want to and not having to ask permission is also valuable. I have known more than a few attorneys who had planned vacations only to have those plans ruined by their boss at the last minute. Imagine: Your boss walks into your office and says he needs you to work next week. You tell him you have been looking forward to an amazing trip with your family for a year. Your boss tells you that you can look forward to looking for work if you don't show up next week, end of conversation. I am able to take all the vacations and trips that I want. Obviously, I know that if I am out of town I am not making money, but the decision is mine and that's the whole point.

Another advantage is that you decide what direction your practice goes in. When I started taking on major felonies cases I didn't have to run the idea by my boss to get his permission. Also, when I gave up my old office I didn't have to ask anyone permission. Having control over little things is nice, but having control over larger decisions is the real benefit. When I decided I wanted to devote more of my time to teaching there was no approval form my boss that I had to get, because I don't have a boss.

If I ever decided that I wanted to work part time, for example, the decision would be mine and no one else's. If I ever decided that I didn't want to do criminal defense work and wanted to do something completely different, I could. Try going to your boss at a bankruptcy firm and tell him you want to start doing nothing but environmental protection work. The last point transitions into the next benefit, which is job security.

I will never get fired and I know this for a fact. For me, this has great value. My practice may slow down or I may have less clients. I may choose to close my practice or my practice could go out of business but I will never have someone walk into my office and tell me that I longer have a job with a firm. If you are the new attorney at a firm and times get tough, the firm has to cut costs... guess who is getting fired? In this recent economy, many firms have downsized and entire departments have been laid off.

Living in Arizona, I know of firms laying off their entire real estate departments. I know of attorneys having little or no notice before being fired. A partner at a firm is never going to lay herself off; they will always find someone below them on the corporate ladder. Again, with my own practice I know there will be good years and slow years but I will never get fired.

What attracted me the most to having my own practice is also potentially the biggest drawback. I loved that I was starting with nothing and trying to grow something from scratch. Some people would view this as a negative. It's obviously harder to build something from nothing as opposed to something from something. I loved knowing that I am solely responsible for the success of my practice. If I bring in a big client or a big case, the entire reward goes to me and no one else.

There is nothing wrong with not wanting to build your own business. As I mentioned earlier, you must be honest with yourself when deciding if you want to have your own practice. If building something out of nothing does not appeal to you, having your own practice is not for you.

I never liked the idea that when you work for a firm, ultimately, you are making money for someone else. Even though the firm may be paying you a decent salary, this doesn't change the fact that someone above you is making more money than you off of your hard work. Some people are not bothered by this concept, but I am.

The issue is not only about money, but also reputation. *If* you work hard and do all the right things, the firm you work for benefits from your work. I like the idea of the rewards of my hard work going to me and no one else. This may sound selfish, but to me it's not about selfishness but about the person who did the work getting the reward. The beauty is in the simplicity. If you run a good practice, you do well; if you don't run a good practice, you don't do well.

I still have many days that I have a hard time believing that I get to do what I do for a job. I really like what I do and I love working for myself. I love going on vacation when I want to, I love the flexibility, and I love knowing that I am building something out of nothing. There are obviously many advantages to having your own practice, but I would not be honest if I did not talk about the disadvantages. Some of the disadvantages I knew about before starting my own practice; others I have learned about along the way.

ADVANTAGES OF WORKING FOR A FIRM AND DISADVANTAGES OF WORKING FOR YOURSELF

Having your own practice is not for everyone, and you have to be honest with yourself if it is something for you. One of the advantages of working for someone else is the support that is available to you. Just today I was talking to an attorney about how I was having a problem with my QuickBooks accounting software. He told me his firm had a person that did all the billing and finance. As I work for myself, I do all the accounting myself. I do everything on my own, which cuts down on overhead but increases the responsibilities I have to worry about, whereas someone at a firm generally only has to focus on clients.

Having a person do all of the finance work is one advantage of working for someone else and just one example of the benefits you get at a firm that you normally don't have when you are on your own. I could go out and hire someone to do all my finances, but that would cut into my profit and, for me, it's not worth hiring someone. Firms may offer logistical support such as an assistant, help with research, and other services. I know many large firms have their own print department for making document copies and transcripts.

Medium or large firms may offer other benefits that a solo practice may not. Firms often offer benefits ranging from health insurance to retirement and others. I know several attorneys at large firms that have expense accounts for cell phones, trips, lunches, dinners, and other fun incidentals. I know one attorney that told me that when he was at a large firm and he had to work during the evening, the firm would pay for takeout from any restaurant in the city and have the food delivered to the office. The same attorney told me that he had several paid trips to conferences. If having some of the benefits I spoke about is important to you, working for a large or medium size firm may be for you.

For some attorneys, the prestige of working for a large firm is alluring. For some it gives them a sense of identity. I think to *some* of these people, being associated with a prestigious firm means they are successful attorneys, however, being at a big, reputable firm does not mean that an attorney is necessarily competent or skilled. If having the security of having a big firm name behind you is important, perhaps having your own firm is not for you.

One of the other disadvantages of having your own practice versus working for a firm or agency is that there are many ethical pitfalls that a young or inexperienced attorney can fall into. There are several reasons a solo attorney may be more at risk. The first reason is that when you are on your own there is no one checking your work. You can have another attorney look over your work, but realistically you won't have someone else checking all of your work like you might at a firm.

Another reason that solo attorneys are more at risk is that many, if not all, large firms have an entire department or boards or committees devoted to ethics. If an attorney is not sure how to go about doing something, he can go to the person or committee at the firm and get the answer. For obvious reasons, this is a definitive advantage of being at a firm. One last ethical disadvantage of being in a solo practice arises if the solo attorney is new and not experienced.

When an attorney is new, it is often difficult to know what the ethical rules say about a certain issue or how to deal with a specific situation. As an attorney becomes more experienced he has the same situations arise over time and it becomes easier to deal with situations when they come up. As with anything, the more you do something, the easier it becomes. At a firm you can go to a different attorney or your supervising attorney and get guidance on an ethics questions or a situation, whereas when you are solo you are more or less on your own.

Lack of funding can be another major disadvantage of being a solo as opposed to working at a firm. One of the main reasons any new business fails is a lack of capital, as well as under-estimating how much money a business will need to get by. A law practice is no different in that it needs capital to survive. This book will cover firm funding at length later on, but you don't need a business degree to know that money will have to come from somewhere.

When a practice is started, the person starting it must know that if he does not have enough money to keep the lights on, the business will be forced to close. The obvious advantage of being at a firm is that someone has already built the firm. You not only have access to all of the firm's resources, but you don't have to worry about the firm running out of money. This is another place where knowing yourself is very important. Are you good at managing money? Are you good at budgeting and planning? If not, how realistic is it for you to manage your firm's finances? The formula is simple; if more money goes out than comes in: GAME OVER.

One last disadvantage that is important to discuss has to do with isolation and a lack of contact with other attorneys. At a firm there are other associate attorneys, managing attorneys, paralegals, assistants, tech support people, and all the other people you see at an office. Everyone interacts, and friendships and relationships are formed. When you are a solo you, are on your own.

If you spend a lot of time in court, as I do, you see other attorneys, but you still spend most of your time on your own in an office or at home. Many attorneys now work from home and may feel isolated. Many attorneys do not mind being on their own, but it's still worth thinking about. I like being around other attorneys, but I also like being on my own, so working by myself is not a problem. I also share an office with two other attorneys, which helps. Office sharing arrangements will be discussed at length later on. If being around other people is important to you, a firm or an agency job may be worth thinking about, though there are ways to establish networks to combat a feeling of isolation.

Technology has helped attorneys stay in touch. Many attorneys belong to listservs where ideas and thoughts are exchanged. There are many different types of listservs. Some are geared for one type of law, while others are geared for a type of practice. For example, there may be a listserv for bankruptcy attorneys or criminal defense attorneys. There are also listservs for solo practitioners.

Some of the listservs are local while others are national or regional. Some of the lists are open to everyone, while others are by invitation only. Like everything, some of the lists are more useful than others. Some are nothing more than a place for attorneys to gossip, while some are wonderfully useful for motions, ideas, and discussions.

CHAPTER 6
SO YOU'VE DECIDED TO
START YOUR OWN PRACTICE
—NOW WHAT?

WHERE TO LOCATE YOUR PRACTICE

This seems like an obvious question, but it is an important one. If you are in a location that you like, you should stay there. The decision is harder if you are in a geographic location where the economy is bad. I went to law school in Michigan, and I knew that if I had stayed in Michigan it would have been harder to start my practice there. It is no secret that Michigan's economy is not doing very well. Starting any business in an economically depressed area makes it that much harder. I understand some people are not able to move for different reasons. If you are in a position where you can move and want to move, it is at least something to think about.

There are several scenarios where you might want to think about moving. You might be in a small town where there is not a big need for attorneys. You may be in a town with a bad economy. Another option is that you simply want to move; there is nothing wrong with this. When deciding if you should move to a different area to practice, there are several things to consider.

The main thing to think about is where you will most likely be happy. The main reason you should be starting your own practice is because you think you will be happier working for yourself. If you are not happy with where you are located, you will never be happy. This is not a difficult concept. If you hate the cold, you should not start your practice in Minnesota. If you hate humidity, Florida is probably not for you. I use the weather as an example, but there are many factors to consider.

Remember that there is at least one downside to starting somewhere new, and I know this first hand. When you move somewhere new, you don't have any contacts. You generally will not have any work contacts or personal contacts. When my wife and I moved to Arizona, we knew we would be starting from scratch. We were okay with starting over because we wanted to live in Arizona. If you are not in a city you want to be in, you will have to decide if moving is worth it. For us, it was worth it and we are glad we did. I have a very good friend who came to my Law Office and Management class and told my students they should move to where the jobs are. I think my friend makes a good point. Think of where the jobs are and where you will be happy, and move if you need to.

If you are going to move to a different city there are a number of factors to consider. For example:

- Proximity to family (if you want to be close to family, not everyone does)
- Strength of the local job market (is the city in an economically depressed area?)
- Number of attorneys already in the area (the more people practicing the more competitive the market will be)
- How much you like/dislike the city (you want to be somewhere where you will be happy)
- The affordability of the city (or lack of affordability)
- Will your husband/wife like the city (if your significant other is not happy, how likely are you to be happy?)
- Is this a place you want to be in for a long time (moving cities is not easy)

ONE FIELD OR MANY FIELDS OF LAW

One of the first decisions you will have to make is whether to focus on one type of law or practice several different types. Obviously, there are advantages and disadvantages to both. The advantage to practicing several areas of law is that you will be more marketable to clients. If someone comes to you to do a business contract and then needs someone for a divorce, and you practice both, you have gained two cases out of one client. When you only practice one area of law, you will often have to turn potential clients away. When a client asks you if you can help with his case, and that case is an area of law you don't practice, that is money walking out your door.

Another advantage to practicing more than one area of law is that there is more variety to your work. Do you enjoy focusing on one type of work or do you prefer a bigger variety in your work? If you decide to practice more than one area of law, you have to then decide if you will do a little of everything or focus on two or three areas of law. Some areas make sense to do together. For example, in Phoenix it makes sense for someone to practice immigration law and criminal law, as the two are often related.

One of the attorneys in my office has built a successful immigration practice after initially only doing criminal work. He realized that many of the clients he was representing in criminal matters needed help with their immigration matters as well. My friend realized that he could turn away a lot of work or he could learn immigration law and keep the clients. Now he benefits from his knowledge in two ways. He is not only able to help his criminal clients with immigration matters, but he can also help his immigration clients with criminal matters. My friend was able to build a successful practice doing two types of law and I think two is the most someone can practice while still having a mastery of those areas.

Today the law and the practice of law are more complex than ever. A competent attorney must stay up to date on current cases, court trends, case trends, and so on. A competent attorney must attend seminars and continuing legal education seminars to stay current. For example, in Arizona the DUI laws change almost every year. The amount of mandatory jail, fees, and interlock requirements all change and a competent attorney must stay on top of all of the changes. All fields of law are in a constant change of flux. I think an attorney can stay current on two fields of law at most. I think practicing three areas is possible, but I would not suggest more than two.

There are several reasons I believe it is best for a new attorney starting his or her own practice to focus on one area of law. First, when you are new, there is very little that you know and much more that you don't. I think it's easier and a more efficient use of your time to attempt to master one field of law. I have been practicing nothing but criminal law for close to four years now, and I still feel there are a ton of things I don't know.

The second reason solos are better off focusing on one area of law is that today most clients want to go to an attorney that focuses one area of law. In other words, most clients want a specialist. Think of it as looking for a doctor. You need a surgery and you have to find a doctor to perform the surgery. Do you want to go to a general practitioner who does a little bit of surgery, or would you rather go to a surgeon who does nothing but the exact surgery that you need? I have had more than a few clients tell me that the reason they hired me was because I practice nothing but criminal law, as opposed to a different attorney that does a little bit of everything.

I chose to focus on criminal law right from the start. I wanted to learn the field well and focus my attention and energy on learning one thing thoroughly. I knew that by focusing on one area of law I would be losing some potential clients who would want to hire me for something else. Over the years I have had potential clients come to me for personal injury cases or civil work, and I have told them that I only do criminal work. When you are new and in need of work it is hard to turn away paying clients, but I wanted to stick with my plan and focus on one area. Criminal law, like all fields of law, has a lot of variety within the field. There is juvenile law, misdemeanor law, appeals, post-conviction work, felonies, drug cases, and vehicular cases, to name a few. Simply because you are focusing on one area of law does not mean you are doing the same thing over and over. I have handled thousands of cases, but I continue to be presented with new challenges and issues. I know criminal defense attorneys that do nothing besides DUI's or only handle juvenile criminal matters. I like doing misdemeanor and felony work because I like the variety, but every lawyer is different.

WHERE TO GET MONEY FOR YOUR PRACTICE

If you are independently wealthy when starting your own practice you will have an easy road. However, I figure close to zero people reading this book are independently wealthy, so you will have to figure out where to get money to start your practice. There are many ways to get money, but not all of the options are good for new attorneys.

There are traditional lenders, like banks and credit unions. The problem with traditional lenders is that they are hesitant to lend to new businesses. When I was starting my practice in 2009, there was a recession going on, so banks were even more hesitant to lend than they usually are. The advantage you have as a solo practitioner when asking a bank for money is that you are likely going to be asking for less money than a bigger business, which makes the lender less nervous. If you are asking for a loan to start a restaurant or another type of business that requires a lot of inventory, you will need more money. To start a law practice your requirements will be a lot simpler. Don't forget, simple is good.

If you do want to borrow money from a traditional lender, consider taking out a loan in your own name versus in the business's name. The bank may be more likely to lend money to a person rather than to a new business. Obviously, your credit score will play a large part in deciding if the bank will lend to you and, if they do, at what interest rate. When considering banks, talk to different ones and find one that treats you well. When I was looking for a bank, some banks were dismissive and condescending, which obviously meant I was not interested in them.

Another lending option is the Small Business Administration (SBA). More information can be found about the agency at their website, www.sba.gov. As the name implies, they are a federal government agency designed to lend money to new businesses. One advantage of the SBA over banks or credit unions is that they generally charge a lower interest rate. One downside to the SBA is that they will take a long time to approve or deny your loan. Remember, you are dealing with the federal government, and things take a long time. If you are applying for an SBA loan, you need to know that the process will likely take months, and you have to plan accordingly. Another aspect to consider with the SBA is that they will require a lot of paperwork, from long applications to business plans that you will need prepared.

One option that I would recommend to others is a business credit card. I knew that I would only need a couple thousand dollars to get me going. I also knew that banks would not be interested in lending that little amount of money. A few different banks explained to me that when it comes to business loans, they are not very interested in small amounts. Because of all the paperwork that the bank must complete, it is not really in their interest to lend small amounts. I found a credit card that had a zero percent APR for the first year and a low APR after that. I was essentially getting an interest-free loan. With credit cards it is important to remember to be careful about ballooning APRs. Be wary, when you are swiping a piece of plastic, it often doesn't feel like you are spending real money; it is easy to let the balance pile up.

When looking for money, don't forget about your family. If your parents or other relatives have a little bit of money to lend you at no interest or low interest, this is not a bad idea. Family members will often be excited about investing in you and your business. Of course, there are also downsides when borrowing from family. First, if you lose money and become unable to reimburse your family, it can be embarrassing and put a strain on your relationships. Another possible downside is that your family may keep reminding you of how you needed their help to get started. I never considered borrowing money from my relatives, because it was important to me to do everything on my own. However, there is nothing wrong with going to family for help.

The last place I would consider looking into for money is a special interest lender. If you belong to a religious group, ethnic group, minority group, or club, you should do some research to see if they offer interest-free or low-interest loans. These types of loans often require a co-signer, so you may have to find someone who trusts you enough to co-sign. For example, in Phoenix there is an organization called Jewish Free Loans that gives interest-free loans to Jewish people starting a business. If you can qualify for an interest-free loan, you will be better off than if you have to worry about paying interest for years.

HOW MUCH MONEY SHOULD YOU HAVE BEFORE STARTING?

There is no simple answer. One size does not fit all. The amount of money you need depends on the type of practice that you want to have. The location of the practice will also dictate how much money you will need before starting. A practice in Manhattan will require more money than a practice in a small town. If you plan on having associates and/or a staff, you will need more money. Also, you need to consider if you are going to work from home or have an office. Will it be an inexpensive office or a luxurious office? While there is no simple answer, below are some guidelines to keep in mind.

You must to have enough money to afford the essentials, like keeping lights on and the doors open. Some people will tell you that you need a year's worth of operating capital (how much money you would need to keep the lights on and the doors open for a year). Other people will tell you six months, while others will say three. My open philosophy is that the more money you save up, the better, but you should have at least enough money to keep the doors open for a couple of months. You should figure that when you first begin your practice you will have very few clients.

In order to estimate how much capital you will need to start your practice, you should add up how much it will cost to run your business for one month and then multiply that amount by the number of months you can survive without making a profit. For example, if your monthly operating budget is one thousand dollars and you want to have enough for three months, you should have $3,000 saved up. If you encounter an expense that you pay annually, like bar dues, you can divide the total by twelve to get an idea of how much the expense is per month. If bar dues are $350 a year, the monthly cost is about $29.

Remember, in the real world you always end up spending more than you expect. This is just the reality of running a business. There will always be unexpected expenses. When I started my own practice, I ended up paying hidden fees to my credit card processing company. In this process, you should consider the following expenses:

- Office expenses (home office or traditional office)
  - Rent
  - Furniture
  - Utilities (in really cold or really hot places, utilities can be incredibly expensive)
  - Hardware (server, computer, printer)
  - Software (including client and finance management)
  - Internet and phone costs
    - Business line
    - Cell phone
    - Messaging service
  - Legal service subscriptions, such as WestLaw
  - FedEx, postage
  - Stationery
    - Business cards
    - Letterhead, envelopes
    - Greeting cards
  - Office supplies
    - Paper
    - Pens
    - Notebooks

- File supplies
  - Kitchen supplies, coffee
- Taxes
  - State
  - Federal
  - Other
- Bar dues
- Insurance
  - Malpractice insurance
  - Health insurance
  - Disability insurance
- Support staff
  - Salaries
  - Worker's compensation
  - Retirement
  - Bonuses
  - Insurance
- Personal expenses
  - Rent/mortgage/HOA dues
  - Utilities
  - Cable and internet
  - Food
  - Travel, entertainment
  - Car
    - Gas
    - Car payments
    - Parking
    - Car registration
    - Maintenance and upkeep

I include living expenses as part of your business because you not only have to keep your practice lights on, you also have to keep your home lights on. If you have a family and have a significant other that is working, this will help with your living expenses. When I started my practice, my wife was working, which covered a lot of our living expenses. Obviously, some of you will not have a working significant other, so you will need to budget all your business expenses and personal expenses.

The list is by no means exhaustive, but more of a starting point for costs to consider when deciding how much money you will need. Your costs will vary, depending on many factors. Some of your variables will be: Is your car paid off, or are you still making payments? Are you going to have a virtual office, a traditional office, or work from home? Can you find inexpensive used furniture, or are you going to spend thousands on new furniture? When I started my practice, my monthly operating budget was about $400 a month. I had almost no savings but I had my zero interest credit cards that I knew would keep me afloat for at least six months. A good general rule is to borrow as little as you can. Always remember that every dollar you borrow you will have to pay back, usually with interest.

Solo or Partner?

There are several advantages to having a partner. First, you are not going at it alone. You have someone on the journey with you. When you have a partner there is always someone there to bounce ideas off of, to cover court appearances for you, and to help out in general. There is also a psychological advantage to knowing that you are not facing the daunting task of starting a law practice on your own. Another great benefit of having a partner is cost sharing. Instead of paying for an entire office, you are paying for half of an office. Instead of paying for a copier, you are paying for half of a copier, and so on.

Although there are benefits to having a partner, I think there are more drawbacks. I never considered having a partner and am glad I was on my own. One of the biggest problems when you are starting out with a partner is that there is usually not enough work for one person, much less two people. Author and law office management guru, Jay Foonberg, once wisely said that two people can starve just as quickly as one. If there is not enough work for one person there will not be enough for two.

Another problem with partnerships is that they are a lot like a marriage, and we know that over half of marriages do not survive. I once had a civil attorney tell me that he spends more time with his law partner than he does with his wife. This makes it extremely important to work with someone who you get along with. He also told me he has fights with his law partner just like he has with his wife. If you and your partner have a falling out, consider how the business will be divided. Who will get the clients, the building, and so on?

I remember learning something in my Business Organizations class in law school that seems to be true. It is not a matter of whether a partnership will fail, but when. I have seen a lot of practices fall apart because the partners could not get along and had different goals. Remember, when you are on your own and you want the practice to go in a different direction, there is no problem. When you have a partner, the two of you need to agree. The more people involved, the more opinions and the more opportunity to disagree.

There are many reasons that partners can have a falling out. Commonly, one partner will want the practice to go in one direction and the other will want something completely different. I knew two attorneys that started a practice and broke up the partnership within the year. One of the attorneys wanted to do felony cases, work hard, and conquer the world. The other partner wanted to do a lot of misdemeanor work, go on a lot of vacations, and spend little time in the office.

Difference in work ethic is another cause for disagreement between partners. If one partner is working 70 hours a week and the second partner is working 30 hours a week, with the money being divided 50/50, how long will that partnership last? If one partner has three kids and is constantly taking time off for school events and other activities while the other partner has no kids and never misses work, what is the future of the business?

Regardless, I know many attorneys that have had productive long-term relationships with their legal partners. Many partners have found success by keeping the money and fees separate. I would recommend anyone thinking about having a partner to consider this option. Even if you have a partner to share expenses with, you can still keep the money separate. If you have an "eat what you kill" style of arrangement, then each person can still work as much or as little as they want without it affecting the other partner.

Attorneys who have successful partnerships must talk about the vision they have for the practice. Talking to a prospective partner initially in order to find out if you are on the same page is much more preferable to starting a practice only to *then* realize you have different goals. Many things must be discussed in detail. Some points to consider talking about are:

- How will the firm's money be divided?
- Will there be separate bank accounts?
- What will be the focus of the firm?
- How much vacation will each partner get?
- How will fees be split?
- Who will pay for what?
- How many hours a week will each partner work?
- Who will handle what part of the practice?
- Who will pay the bills?
- Who will bring in the clients?
- Who will travel for distant court dates?
- Who will make management decisions?
- Who will handle personnel issues?
  - o Who will handle the hiring and firing?
  - o Who will be in charge of employee discipline?
- Who will handle trials?
- Who will do appeals?
- How long will the partners want to be in the partnership?
- How much advertising will there be?
  - o Who will decide on advertising costs and how the advertising is done?
- How big or small will the firm be?
  - o What if one person wants to expand and the other one does not?

After talking about everything, there must be a partnership agreement. Think of it as prenuptial agreement. No one gets married hoping to get divorced, but it's a good idea to be prepared. The partnership agreement must include information like how the firm will be dissolved, if one partner wants to buy out the other partner, what the procedure will be, and what each partner is responsible for. Many partnership agreements can be found online. The best idea, however, is to go to a business attorney and have him draft the agreement for you.

After the agreement is drafted, have each partner take the agreement to their own attorney for review. You will spend a little money paying for an attorney to draft the partnership agreement, but you will potentially save yourself a lot of stress down the road. Make sure your partner is someone you know and trust. I have heard too many sad stories of partners stealing money from each other, being deceitful, and so on. You may be spending more time with your partner than with your spouse, so make sure it is someone you like, someone you can work with, and someone you trust. Remember, you are looking for someone that you can work with, but also see daily and spend a significant amount of time with. You are not looking for a friend, but someone you can build a business with.

DIFFERENT OFFICE OPTIONS

First, you will need to decide if you want an office and, if so, what type. A traditional office is not necessary for new attorneys, mainly because of the cost. Say you find a great deal on an office for $400. $400 a month for an actual office in most markets is not realistic, but it will work for our example. You may think $400 a month is easily affordable. The problem with this logic is that when you are starting out, $400 is a lot. Even if you are able to pay for the office, you are still wasting money. Over a year you are spending $4,800 that you don't have to be spending. Those funds could be going into your pocket or be reinvested into the practice.

The type of practice you have will also dictate if an office is necessary. If you have a criminal defense practice, meeting clients at the courthouse is not a problem. Before I had a physical office, I would often meet clients at the courthouse and no one ever seemed to mind. I think some clients even preferred this method, because for them it was the equivalent of meeting a surgeon in an operating room. If you have an estate-planning firm, you will have to meet with clients and will probably need to have an office. A home office is also an option that we will discuss soon.

The type of client you are trying to attract will also dictate the need for an office. If your specialty is banking law, and most of your clients are corporate executives, you must have an office. You can't meet a CFO of a bank at a Starbucks and tell him or her you don't have an office. Certain clients expect certain offices, because an office is a reflection of the attorney. If you are trying to present an exclusive, elite image to tackle high-priced clients, your office must reflect that image.

I encourage young attorneys to begin without an office because it simplifies your life in several ways. Think of all the bills you won't have to worry about every month, as well as all of the headaches that go along with keeping up an office. Those of you who own houses know that something is always breaking and needing repair, and an office is no different. Offices have maintenance issues, such as electrical, heating, technology, and plumbing problems. Not having an office can also save time and money on commuting. If you are able to work from home, think of the time you can save by staying home instead of driving to your office. If you are located in large city with heavy traffic, not commuting can be a big advantage.

Some attorneys are worried about not having a traditional office because they fear that a client will think less of them if clients find out they don't have a real, physical office. I recommend that attorneys tell clients that you are saving them money by not having an office. Working from home or having a virtual office allows you to charge the client less, because your overhead is less. Young attorneys must also understand that most clients don't care if you have an office. Clients understand that current attorneys are more mobile than ever and that an entire practice can be run from a smartphone. Do not be embarrassed if you choose to forgo an office. Turn a negative into a positive and explain to the client how they benefit from you being without an office. If you decide you need an office, there are several options.

THE TRADITIONAL OFFICE

The most traditional office option is paying someone to rent office space. The office can be in a small building with only a couple of spaces or in a large high-rise with hundreds of offices. The rooms themselves can range from under a hundred feet to many thousand feet. If you decide on a traditional office you need to discover how much space you require. The less space you need, the less money you will have to spend. Many places charge by square footage, so more space means more money. A perfect office should have enough space to make you comfortable, but not so much that it causes you to waste money or it makes the office feel empty.

Offices can come furnished or unfurnished. A furnished office will cost more, but will typically save time because you will not have to purchase furniture. If you have an unfurnished office and need furniture, consider buying used. Used furniture will cost much less than new furniture, and when you are starting fresh, every penny counts. If you have extra furniture at home or know of someone interested in donating office equipment, consider this option instead of buying new or used.

When you start looking for an office, you must do research. The process is similar to renting an apartment or a house—you need to check the place out. Some things to consider when choosing an office:

- How close is the office to your home?
- How is parking?
- How close is the office to the courthouse you use most?
- How safe is the neighborhood?
- Will clients like the neighborhood?
- Will clients like the building?
- How clean is the office?
- How long is the lease?
- What utilities are included?
- What time in the evening does the heat or AC get turned off?
- How often does the office get cleaned?
- Is there a kitchen or kitchenette?

Another good idea when visiting an office building is to talk to some of the other tenants. If the building manager is reputable, they will be glad to give you contact information for past and current tenants. If the building manager does not want you speaking to other renters, this is a red flag and you should walk away. By questioning other tenants, you will get a good feel for the building. Ask the current tenants if they enjoy working with the building management, if they like the space, and what (if any) complaints they have. The more information you acquire, the better-informed decision you will be able to make.

It is important to know from whom you are renting, especially if you are subletting. I almost learned this lesson the hard way. When I was starting out I met an attorney who seemed really friendly. She had an office to sublet and told me the office was $1000 per month. I learned that $1000 for that office was a terrible price, but she made it seem like a great deal. I had a bad feeling about the whole arrangement and ended up walking away. The attorney tried to convince me by explaining how the office would practically pay for itself and how I would generate a large profit by having the office. After I walked away I realized that the attorney had a terrible reputation and many people had problems with her. If I had gone through with the arrangement, I am pretty sure the rent would have put me out of business and my firm would not have survived.

The point is that if you do get an office, do all of your research and be sure you know what you are getting yourself into. If you don't have all of the necessary information, walk away. Think of the movies that have the cliché where the star gets a bad feeling and doesn't commit the crime because he realizes it's a setup and the cops are waiting. Unfortunately, some landlords and other attorneys will take advantage of young, inexperienced attorneys.

WORKING FROM HOME

Today, more and more attorneys choose to work from home. In the past, there was a stigma against attorneys working from home. The widespread belief was that a "real" lawyer needed an office. Many of those attitudes are shifting as technology and society advance. I know more than a few successful attorneys that have a home office with no interest in getting a traditional office. There are several advantages to working from home. One of the biggest is saving money on an office. You save money not only from not paying for a separate office space, but also on taxes. A home office can be a deduction that any knowledgeable accountant can tell you about.

A home office can also be a good way to save time. You won't need to drive to and from the office, thus eliminating a commute. Another benefit is that if you have kids, it can be a lot easier to monitor the children while working at home. One aspect to think about is the genre of your clients and whether you are willing to allow them into your home. I have a criminal defense practice, so a client coming to my house is out of the question. If you have an estate planning practice, however, you may agree to clients knowing where you live and visiting your home.

If your office is located in your home, remember that you are not required to invite your client in. Many attorneys will use a friend's office or meet clients at coffee shops or restaurants. A lot of documents can now be shared via the Internet, so now less face-to-face meetings are required than in the past. Something else to consider with a home office, if you are having clients come to the house, is will your homeowners insurance protect you? A good idea is to check your homeowners insurance to see what is protected. For example, if a client injures himself in your home, will you be covered?

One other factor worth checking is if the local zoning laws permit you to run a business out of your home. Zoning laws or local HOA rules may not allow you to have clients come to your house. A more efficient method is to check the local laws before starting your office at home rather than to set up the entire office and find out it is prohibited.

VIRTUAL OFFICE

There are several variations of a virtual office. One option provides a service that answers your phone calls and takes messages. Some services forward your calls to a cell phone or a landline (if anyone still has a landline). Other virtual offices have meeting spaces or day offices that can be rented. Virtual offices can be a good option for attorneys who want the appearance of an actual office without having to pay for one. Some attorneys like virtual offices as a second location if they are trying to expand their practice with a second office. As more attorneys realize traditional offices are unnecessary, virtual offices are becoming more popular. Most major cities will have no shortages of virtual offices. They vary in price and location just as traditional offices do. Again, you must do your research and know what you are looking for.

When I started my practice I had a virtual office and it suited me well. I found an office building close to my house that offered virtual office services. For about 200 dollars a month, the office would sign for my mail, forward my calls to my cell and, if I didn't answer, they would take a message for me. When someone called my office, an actual person would answer the phone and the computer would tell him the client was calling for me, so he would answer the phone as if he was my own receptionist. I enjoyed that it appeared as if I had my own receptionist while I was paying a fraction of the cost.

Another great service that my office offered was that they had conference rooms and day offices that I could rent by the hour. If I ever wanted to meet a client in the office or the conference room, I would just reserve a space and then, when a client came in, I would meet him or her in the conference room. As with everything, there are some drawbacks to virtual offices.

Some virtual offices are very expensive and in my opinion not worth the cost. Another issue with virtual offices is they are not real offices, so if you want to use an actual office without paying by the hour, you are out of luck. Something else to watch out for with virtual offices is the length of the contract. Many virtual offices will want you to sign long-term contracts. If the office is satisfactory, a long-term contract may be acceptable, but unfortunately you may not discover problems until you have signed the contract, and by then it is too late. Some things to consider when looking for a virtual office:

- Length of contract?
- Do other customers of the virtual office like the place?
- What is the penalty for violating the lease?
- Does the location have an actual, physical office that can be used?
- Parking?
- Internet?
- Printing services?
- Is everything one price, or are there extra charges for phone answering?
- What hours will the phone be answered?
- Where do after-hour phone calls go?
- Will a local receptionist be answering your calls or will they go to a call center overseas?
- How late in the evening does the A/C or heat work?
- Location of the virtual office?
- Are there any hidden costs?

Overall, I think a virtual office can be a great option for a new law practice. When you are starting out, controlling costs is probably the biggest factor that will determine if your practice succeeds or fails. A virtual office can help control costs while giving the appearance of an actual office.

OFFICE SHARING

There is a variety of office sharing arrangements. The two most common are where either the attorney subletting the office pays rent to the attorneys who own the office or the new attorney does some work in exchange for the office space. One of the biggest advantages to an office sharing arrangement is that other attorneys are around to offer mentorship and answer questions. Another advantage is the aspect of cost sharing. Instead of paying for everything on your own, the cost is divided between all of the attorneys. For example, if there are three attorneys, the costs are split three ways.

When I gave up my virtual office after having it for about eighteen months, I moved in with two attorneys that both practiced criminal defense work. Our arrangement was that they would not charge me rent and, in return, I would make some court appearances on their behalf. It was beneficial for both of us, because they had an extra empty office and would be getting some free work out of me while I got a rent-free office and, more importantly, would have two resources to go to with questions. I have been at the office for close to three years now and our arrangement still works well for everyone.

Something to keep in mind with office sharing arrangements is that clients must understand that you have your own practice and are not in a firm with the other attorneys. An office sharing arrangement can be confusing for clients because there are several attorneys in an office, which can look like a firm. The client must clearly know that they are hiring you, and only you, not the other attorneys in the office. A good idea is to have a line or two in your fee agreement that states you are not associated with the other attorneys in the office and only you will be working on the client's case. While considering office sharing arrangements, there are some things to think about:

- What is included in the arrangement?
  - Receptionist service (if there is a receptionist, how will the phone be answered?)
  - Postage?
  - Parking?
  - Utilities?
  - Who pays for office expenses?
    - Printer
    - Phone
    - Computer
    - Fax
    - Internet
    - Heat or A/C
    - Coffee/water services?
  - Cleaning services?
  - Who decides when the arrangement is terminated?
  - Is there a written lease?

- If the office wants to buy something new, how is the decision to purchase or not to purchase made?
- If the tenants want to move, how will moving decisions be handled?

One last factor to consider is how well you know the attorneys you are sharing the office with. Before I began my office sharing arrangement I asked my lawyer friends about the attorneys I was thinking of sharing an office with. I knew the attorneys in the office a little but I talked to a lot of people that knew them well. Only after I felt comfortable that the attorneys were reputable did I feel comfortable moving into their office. Like everything else, it is easier to do your research up front rather than have problems after you have moved in.

P.O. BOX/SUITE

One last aspect to take into account when choosing your office is to consider having a P.O. box. Many attorneys that have home offices have a P.O. box for receiving services. The advantage to a P.O. box is that you can have a home office without giving your home address to clients. Some mail services will provide you with a P.O. box for rent. They can also give you a box number, and those are called suites. The advantage is that your written address has "suite" instead of "P.O. box" on it. One factor to be wary of with P.O. boxes is that many corporate commissions require a physical address and will not accept a P.O. box. This can be a problem if you desire to form a corporation or an L.L.C.

VISION FOR YOUR PRACTICE

When you start planning your practice, it is important to envision the type of practice you want. Picking the type of law you want to practice is important, but a larger vision of your practice is also necessary. You must think about what type of clients you want to attract, how you plan on growing your practice, and if/when you hope to hire an assistant. Do you want an assistant and/or associates?

The more questions you ask yourself, the better off you will be once you actually start your practice. I remember I spent over one year planning my practice. I spent time planning my office, where I wanted to live, and how I would pay for the practice. I thought about every possibility I could. I knew the more scenarios and possibilities for my practice I ran through in my head, the better off I would be when I actually started my practice. Remember, the more you plan, the better off you will be.

Legal Entity Formation

You must decide what type of entity your practice will be. Most small firms are either L.L.C.s or corporations. Every state has something equivalent to a corporation commission that will have all the forms available on their website. You want to make sure that you form some type of structure, whether it is an L.L.C. or a corporation, to protect yourself. If you do not have an L.L.C. or a corporation, you could be held personally liable in the case of a lawsuit or a judgment. Running your practice through an L.L.C. or corporation can protect you.

Once you submit the paperwork, you need to publish the news of the formation of your company. You can go to an attorney that specializes in formation documents, but you can probably save the money and do it yourself. I remember when I filled out the documents they were confusing, but I got through it. If I can do it, anyone can. If you have a couple hundred extra dollars, going to a corporation attorney is not a bad idea. The attorney can look over your documents and make sure everything is in order.

CHAPTER 7
HOW TO MAKE MONEY

So, you have decided to start your own practice. You have picked a perfect office location. Now comes the hard part. How will you make money and keep the practice afloat? The traditional way law firms make a profit is by having private clients. When you are new, this presents a few problems. First, most clients don't want to be your guinea pig. When you are searching for a surgeon to perform your operation, would you want to be the surgeon's first patient?

A new client may feel more comfortable with a new attorney depending on the type of work you would be doing for them. If you are doing estate planning and someone asks you to create a simple will, they probably won't mind that you are new. However, if someone comes to you to set up three different trusts involving foundations and charities, they probably won't be thrilled to hire someone new. Luckily, clients often do not ask how many cases you have handled. When I was doing my first jury trial, my biggest fear was that the client would ask if I had ever done this before. Thankfully, she never asked that.

The second problem for new attorneys when it comes to attracting clients is that it takes time to build up a client list. Most attorneys will tell you that it takes anywhere from five to ten years of experience before you gain a steady flow of private clients. Once you start getting clients, they come back to you and often refer friends and family, but the process takes time. This is not to say it's impossible to get a large amount of private clients immediately, but it's not typical. While your practice is forming, how does one generate enough money to survive?

COVERING FOR OTHER ATTORNEYS

One of the best ways for new attorneys to make money is unknown by young lawyers. When I started, I knew nothing of this method and had to have it explained to me, as I had no idea what it was. One of my main mentors told me I should "cover" for other attorneys. Covering for an attorney occurs when a lawyer is unable attend a hearing or appear in court, so you go in his place. An attorney may need coverage for a pretrial conference, a settlement conference, a trial, or any other type of courtroom setting. The attorney may be sick, out of town, have a scheduling conflict, forget about a court date, or simply not want to go. I once covered for an attorney that didn't want to reschedule his squash game. There are great benefits for covering for other attorneys.

The first is that you will make money. A coverage attorney will either charge by the hour or have a flat fee per appearance or day. When deciding how much to charge, discuss the local market with other attorneys. The market you are in will dictate what you can charge and what clients will pay. The wages are almost always less than what you would make from a private client, but when you are starting out, private clients will be limited and few and far between.

The second benefit is that you are constantly learning while you are working. When I began covering, I met judges and prosecutors that I practice with and in front of regularly. When you cover you begin to build your reputation. If you are professional, courteous, prompt, and ethical, people will notice. Other attorneys and judges were aware I was new, but they saw that I was trying and hustling, which they respected. You not only get to go to court, but you get paid to go! Many coverage appearances are very simple and require easy tasks, like filing a motion to continue. Sometimes, however, coverage appearances can be complicated and involve cooperating with difficult clients, difficult prosecutors, or difficult judges.

Another benefit of providing coverage is the networking opportunities. You will likely cover for both good and bad attorneys. When you cover for skillful attorneys, you learn the correct way to run a law practice. You learn how to communicate with clients and how to practice properly. When you cover for bad attorneys, you learn what not to do. When I started covering, I didn't know very much about running a practice, so I learned a great deal from both types of attorney.

Coverage opportunities are never advertised, so everything is done by referral and word of mouth. I went from covering for one attorney to covering for well over 100 attorneys in a few years, all by reputation. Attorneys are like clients; if you perform well, they will tell other attorneys, who will in turn hire you. In the legal profession, you have to have connections. You have to know people and people have to know you. Connections and relationships are not made overnight and must be built over time.

Elements to consider when covering for attorneys are plentiful. Some attorneys will intentionally throw you on figurative land mines. They may do it accidently or on purpose. Some attorneys will send you in their place if they know that the judge is mad at them or if there is a problem with the case. Some attorneys will not pay on time, so try to avoid covering for these attorneys as well. When you come across these attorneys, you should avoid covering for them in the future.

I once had to chase an attorney for close to a year to collect fifty dollars. I had covered a pre-trial conference for her and promptly sent her a bill. I will usually give a follow up phone call if an attorney has not paid in about a month. I called her and received no answer, so I left a voice mail. About a month after, I resent the invoice and tried to call again. Almost a year went by with no response from her. I ran into her almost a year later, and kindly informed her that she still owed me money. She did not apologize and wrote me a check. I never covered for her again.

The type of law you practice may potentially limit your coverage opportunities. If you practice bankruptcy, family, or criminal law, opportunities to cover will present themselves, because court appearances are plentiful. If your area of practice provides few court appearances, you will see fewer opportunities. Keep in mind: you can fill in for more than just court appearances. You can cover depositions, interviews, and anything else where an attorney is needed.

Related to coverage, doing legal research for other attorneys is another way to network and earn money. Before I started covering, I did legal research for a number of attorneys. Lawyers like to hire people to do their research for them, because attorneys do not like to do their own research. Many attorneys believe that their time is too valuable to be doing research and that their time can be better spent doing something else. Research can be tedious, but it is one method of getting money.

In order to find attorneys who need help researching, you need to know attorneys who are aware that you are available. When you meet an attorney, let him know that you are available for his legal research needs. If you don't inform people of your availability, they will never know.

CONTRACTS

Almost every city and county will have various contracts available for attorneys. These positions vary, but generally they involve a county or city paying an attorney directly to handle cases. Cities and counties provide contract positions for many reasons. They can be civil or criminal and are an excellent way for attorneys to supplement their income. Contracts can offer more than a little extra income. A number of attorneys make a comfortable living doing just contract work.

Many types of contracts are prevalent in both cities and counties. In criminal practice, there are county, city, and federal contracts. At the federal and county level there are public defender offices, but those offices are often conflicted off cases. There are many ways for an office to be conflicted off a case. One of the most common is if the office has represented a present co-defendant in a previous matter. If an agency is conflicted off a case, private attorneys are brought in and paid directly by the government.

Private attorneys will also be brought in on occasion if there are not enough attorneys at an agency to handle the case load. Contract work generally does not pay as well as private work, but often the work is steady and pays better than no work at all. Most cities, including Phoenix, do not have a traditional public defender's office employing full-time attorneys. The city of Phoenix, like most cities in Arizona, pays private attorneys to handle criminal matters for indigent clients. Contracts are also available for juvenile and guardian work. Many cities will also have civil contracts for civil attorneys. For example, a city may have a contract reviewing proposed contract bids that the city is seeking. Just like criminal contracts, the pay will vary from contract to contract and city to city.

Contracts are often not advertised, but if they are, they are difficult to locate. An advertisement might be buried in some city or county website where no one will ever see it. Like many things in the legal profession, you must have connections that will inform you of when an opening appears. The best way to find out which contracts are available is to talk to an experienced attorney in your area. Some of the contracts require years of experience while others do not.

In general, the people in charge of the contract want to know who they are hiring, so it is beneficial to know the people in charge. A good way to network is to spend time in the court where you are hoping to get a contract. Some cities have agencies that appoint the contracts. In some jurisdictions (mostly small towns) the judge assigns his own cases to local attorneys.

As the economy gets worse, more attorneys become interested in contract positions because they provide job security. When jobs become more difficult to find, competition becomes more common. Currently, I have a contract with the City of Phoenix, and there are always many more applicants than openings. A contract position can be a great way for young attorneys to learn because of the variety the arrangement offers.

FAMILY AS CLIENTS

When you are looking for work, don't forget about your family. If you are practicing in the same city as your family, go to them and ask them if they have any legal needs. I have an attorney friend who has a lot of family members that get arrested, and they always call him for help. Ask them if you can do a simple will for them for a few hundred dollars. You don't have to be an estate-planning attorney to figure out an uncomplicated will. Remember, your family is more likely to trust you when you are new. Often, family will ask you to provide free legal services, and it is your choice. On one hand, they will appreciate your work, but on the other hand, you are not making any money and your family may think you will always provide services free of charge.

Even if your family does not have any work for you, they may have friends that do. Make sure your family is telling people that you have a practice and that you can help with their legal matters. If you are doing estate planning and your parents have older friends, they are potential clients. If you do criminal defense work and you have a brother whose friends are always getting arrested, they are also potential clients.

TEACHING

When you are starting out, consider teaching opportunities. Local community colleges, paralegal schools, and other institutions may be interested in having an attorney teach. Another place to consider is an LSAT or bar prep center. If you received a high score on the bar or the LSAT, companies will probably be interested in hiring you to teach. Many organizations or parents will look for tutors. Tutors will often charge about $20 an hour, which is a lot better than not working.

Today, there are more online schools, and many of the schools are always looking for teachers. Teaching an online class can have the benefit of keeping your schedule free to do other work. Also, often the online teaching positions are easier to get than traditional teaching jobs. I know many experienced defense attorneys that teach online classes to supplement their income. Be creative where you look. Teaching may not be something you are passionate about, but work is work.

BUILDING UP PRIVATE CLIENTELE

The best way to make money in private practice is from private clients. Private clients will pay you more than court-appointed or contract-appointed defendants. The problem with building up a private client practice is that it takes time. Most attorneys build up a private client practice through referrals. The more happy clients you have, the more referrals you will get. Building up referrals takes time, and new attorneys must remember to be patient.

Many experienced attorneys have told me that it takes anywhere from five to ten years to build up a private clientele. Obviously you may get lucky and start getting referrals earlier, but again, remember to be patient. One way to start building up a private clientele is by taking the clients that other attorneys may not want or may not have time for. Talk to attorneys you know and tell them that you would love their referrals. Other attorneys may give you their potential clients for several reasons. For example, the other attorney may be charging more than the client can afford to pay. If the other attorney knows you are new and willing to do the case for less they can give you the referrals. The other attorney may also not want to deal with the client, as they are difficult and/or stubborn. They may have the luxury of turning away the difficult client, but you do not.

When I started I had an attorney refer a case to me in northern Arizona because she did not want to make the drive. I was more than glad to make the drive and made some money in the process. The client in northern Arizona referred me to his roommate, so I got two clients out of one. If you do a good job for your clients, eventually the referrals will come and your private clientele will grow. I have been in private practice for four years and I am just now starting to build up a regular private client base. New attorneys must work on getting referrals but they must also work on keeping current clients.

Some clients will refer you to their friends and some clients will come back to you in later cases. In criminal defense work, many clients get into trouble over and over. If they like their defense attorney they will go to them again. For example, I have had defense attorney friends that have represented the same defendant on three different DUIs. In Civil cases, you may have a client that comes back to the same attorney for different lawsuits or other civil matters.

IMPORTANCE OF HAVING DIFFERENT STREAMS OF INCOME

As an attorney, you should always be careful that your income is never dependent on one source. A good attorney must diversify their sources of income. Anyone that has ever watched an investment show or read how-to books about Wall Street will have heard about the importance of diversification. In a stock market sense, the term means that an investor should have diversity in the types of stock they own. The logic is that if one sector of the economy slows down, only a part of the investor's portfolio will be invested. If an investor does not have a diverse portfolio, they could be wiped out. The same logic applies to attorneys.

If your entire income is dependent on one type of income, and that source of income goes away, you will be in serious trouble. If 100% of your income is one single contract and you lose that contract, your practice will have to close. No matter how profitable one source of income is, you must remember that it can always go away. I have known many defense attorneys that were 100% dependent on private clients. For whatever reason, the private clients dried up. When the private clients dried up, the attorneys had no means of making money.

The more sources of income you have, the more stable your practice will be. In my practice, I have four separate sources of income: (1) I have one contract, (2) private clients, (3) coverage for other attorneys, and (4) being a law professor. I know that I could lose any one at any time, but I would still be okay as I have other sources of income. For me, an attorney who only has one source of income is like rock climbing without a safety rope.

SHOULD YOU ADVERTISE?

There are different attitudes about whether new attorneys should advertise. One viewpoint is that new attorneys must advertise to get new clients. Some attorneys will tell you that even if you have to take out loans to pay for the ads, it is worth it. They will tell you it is worth it because the ads will bring in enough clients to pay for the ads plus you get your name out there.

In my opinion, as new attorneys, you should not advertise. The first reason has to do with cost. Advertising is incredibly expensive. In the Phoenix, Arizona market in 2012, a fifteen second television commercial cost about $300. That $300 is to run the advertisement once. Radio and print commercials cost less but are still very expensive. When you have a new practice you should be counting your pennies, and advertising is not the best use of your money.

The second reason I am not a big advocate of new attorneys advertising is because in order for the advertising to be effective, you must have a lot of ads. I learned this first hand when I ran an ad in the local college paper. The guy selling the ad promised me all kinds of things and the ad was for a quarter of a page and cost $200 dollars a week. The paper had a circulation of about 200,000 people. I figured if I gained one client out from the ad, it would pay off. After running the ad for six weeks, I did not get a single client, a single call. Part of the reason is because no one reads newspapers. If someone does look at a paper, it is in passing.

Another part of the reason the ad produced no clients is because Phoenix has hundreds of criminal defense lawyers, many of whom spend small fortunes on advertising. Between TV, radio, billboards, bus ads, and other types of ads, the legal field does not have a shortage of attorneys. My print in the paper never had a chance against a firm spending tens of thousands and sometimes hundreds of thousands of dollars a month on ads. I am not opposed to advertising, I think if it is done correctly it can produce results. However, for the aforementioned reasons, I generally advise new attorneys to do little to no advertising.

If you are interested in advertising, consider guerrilla marketing/advertising. The term was coined by someone much smarter than me and deals with getting free advertising. Consider contacting a local paper and ask them if you can write a column for them. Contact local TV channels and ask if they ever have some kind of an "Ask a Lawyer" segment that you could come on for.

Another good way to get your name out there for free is with online services that answer legal questions to the general public at no charge. Services like Avvo.com have attorneys that answer people's questions and people can hire an attorney that they find on the website. Avvo does an attorney rating for every attorney who is a member. One of the ways to increase your score is to answer people's legal questions. Answering questions is free and a good way to get your name out there. Avvo, like everyone else, will try to sell you a premium subscription, but the base membership is free. Avvo is just one example and there are many websites like it.

Be creative and think of ways to get advertising. You will have less money than established firms but you will have more creativity and time, which you should use to your advantage. If you think of some clever, free advertising and you try it and it produces no leads, you have not lost anything, because you didn't pay anything.

CHAPTER 8
PROFESSIONALISM

Reputation is everything for a lawyer. This might be the single most important thing I can teach you. Let me say it again in all capital letters. REPUTATION IS EVERYTHING. A good reputation goes with you throughout your entire career. A bad reputation does the same thing. An attorney's reputation affects every part of their practice. How clients, prosecutors, opposing counsel, judges, court support staff, and everyone else you work with view you is affected by your reputation.

Every day I work with attorneys with excellent reputations and with terrible reputations. The attorneys with excellent reputations get better offers from prosecutors, more extensions from judges, better dates from bailiffs, and enjoy many other benefits. The attorneys with terrible reputations get all the opposite. Another thing that's important to remember about reputations is that they are not stagnant. An attorney's reputation is always getting better or getting worse. There is also a snowball effect. If your reputation is getting better, it gets better quicker over time. The same thing is true about a bad reputation.

Young attorneys must remember that they are always being judged and evaluated. Every time you go to court, every time you file a motion, every time you talk with a prosecutor or opposing counsel, you are being judged. The person dealing with you is deciding that they think you are competent, professional, courteous, and pleasant to work with, or you are not. Part of establishing a positive reputation is always being mindful of your own possible arrogance.

I have seen many young—and some not so young—attorneys have their reputation ruined by arrogance. There is nothing worse than when I see a young attorney be rude or arrogant to a staff support person like a bailiff or a clerk, or anyone for that matter. This is close to professional suicide. Lawyers must remember to be humble and to not only not be arrogant, but to not even be perceived as arrogant. In the case of arrogance, perception becomes reality. Arrogance is not to be confused with confidence. A good attorney should be confident and carry himself or herself in a confident manner.

A young attorney must remember that everyone in the legal community talks and most attorneys know each other. Not only do attorneys talk to each other but they also talk to bailiffs, clerks, and judges, and all those people talk to each other. When a young attorney is arrogant to a bailiff in one court, he or she often doesn't realize that the bailiff will not only talk to his judge but to other bailiffs and other attorneys.

I am amazed at how often an interpreter, bailiff, or prosecutor will tell me about what some other attorney did or what they heard that some other attorney did. The lesson in this is that everyone talks. This can either be a benefit or a problem. If you do things right, people will talk about that. If you do things wrong and are arrogant, I can guarantee you people will talk about that.

I know one attorney who started his own practice and things were going well, but at some point he took a wrong turn and become arrogant. He started telling people about how well he was doing and about how successful his practice was. He began to irritate people with his attitude, and soon people began to talk. After a while his reputation was tarnished, and it will be virtually impossible for him to undo that. I would recommend you learn from his experience and not make the same mistake yourself. As everyone knows, it's a lot easier to learn from other people's mistakes then your own.

PUNCTUALITY AND CALENDARING

It seems easy and obvious that attorneys should be on time. Despite this I am amazed how often attorneys show up late. The problem with showing up late is that it annoys people. Being late annoys clients, opposing counsel and, worst of all, judges. If you are running late, always call the court and tell them you are running late. Even if you are only a little late, the court will appreciate the gesture. I am not saying you cannot be thirty seconds or one minute late but if people have to wait for you they will remember it. Some judges are less forgiving about punctuality then others. I have seen more than a few attorneys get yelled at by judges for being repeatedly late. No one enjoys having an angry judge with a courtroom of people watching.

Obviously things will come up and you will be late from time to time. Courts run late, traffic jams happen, and unexpected things come up. As an attorney, part of being professional is to let the court know and to not make a habit of being late. A lot of the time I will have two court settings in the same building at the same time. It is clear that I will not be in the same place at the same time. When I come to court, I go to the second courtroom and tell them I have to be in a different courtroom and will come to the second courtroom as quickly as I can. I will usually also leave my cell phone number with the bailiff so the court can get a hold of me if they need to.

A big part of punctuality is calendaring. Calendaring is the simple practice of writing down dates in a paper or electronic calendar. It is impossible to be a good attorney without keeping a good calendar. There is no perfect way to calendar, but it is something that must be done. The practice is not difficult but one that must be learned early. When you are starting out you may be tempted to just remember dates in your head. This is a terrible idea and must be avoided. Always write down dates. You do not want to be standing in front of an angry judge explaining that you had the court date in your head but forgot.

A calendar is only useful if it is used regularly. Not only must you put all your appointments and court dates into it, you must also check it regularly. I usually check my calendar every evening to make sure I know where I am going in the morning and that I have not forgotten anything. It doesn't matter if you use a traditional paper calendar or an electronic one on your phone or computer, but you must have one.

One of the simplest and best calendar programs is Google Calendar. My favorite aspect of the program is that it automatically updates between devices. You can enter something from your phone and it will show up on your computer. There are much fancier, more expensive programs, but I think they are usually not needed. Google Calendar is free, easy to use, and easy to update. A word of caution about calendar software—calendar software, like all software and computers, sometimes break. I keep an electronic calendar but I also use a good old-fashioned paper calendar. I know the paper calendar will never shut off or delete all my appointments.

GOING TO COURT

In virtually every office or court setting there are people that you want to see and people you don't. The people you don't want to see do nothing but complain. They are not fun to be around. Sometimes they are stressful to be around, and sometimes they are downright unpleasant. Every office and work place in the world has this type of person. People do not like them and talk behind their back about how they do not like them. There is also another type of person in every office.

The second type of person is someone people like to be around. This person is positive, pleasant, polite, and enjoyable to be around. This type of person makes small talk, asks people about their weekends, and remembers people's hobbies. You get the picture. When you go to court you find the same two types of people. Your goal is to be the second type. Your life will be easier and people will do more for you when they like you. Don't be fake and pretend to care, because people can tell. Be polite and friendly. Your goal should be that when someone sees you coming, they smile and look forward to talking to you.

When you got to court, it is important to know your personality. If you are quiet and shy, there is nothing wrong with this. If you are shy and introverted, don't try to be outgoing and boisterous. If you are naturally outgoing and love to talk to people, don't try to be withdrawn. No matter your personality, always be polite, friendly, and the type of person people like to be around. Always be on your best behavior.

When you go to court you must dress like a professional. This seems as obvious as the fact you should be on time, but I am always amazed at what I see attorneys wearing to court. When you are an experienced attorney, people will not judge you on your clothing because they know that you are either competent or you are not. When you are a new attorney, court personal and clients do not know if you are competent. The only thing people in court know about you when you first show up is how you are dressed. If it is your first time in court and you are a female attorney and you show up in a low cut shirt, in a short skirt, and clear heels, what kind of image does that present? You may think I am making up the clear heels, but I have seen a female attorney come to court in clear heels. You can't make this stuff up.

On more than one occasion I have brought female students to court and, after the students left, other attorneys made comments to me about how the students were not dressed appropriately. The attorneys that saw the students didn't know anything about the students but they knew how they were dressed. It is not fair that attorneys are judged on their clothing, but it is a fact of life, so you must plan accordingly. It is also not fair that female attorneys are judged more on their clothing then male attorneys, but this is also a fact. I always tell my students to go out and to spend a little bit of money on nice clothing. When dressing for court, here are some things to keep in mind:

- Are your shoes polished?
- Are you wearing anything that could be perceived as inappropriate?
- Are your shoes appropriate for court?
- Are you clean-shaven?
- Are your pants properly hemmed?
- Do your clothes match?

- Are you wearing a lot of perfume/cologne?
- Is your outfit drawing attention to you?
- Do you look like a professional?
- Do you look like you would want your attorney to look?

A lot of your clothing will depend on what court you are in. For example, in Federal court men and women are expected to wear a jacket. In most of the city courts, a jacket is not required and many attorneys will not wear a jacket. When you are a young attorney and dressing for court, you should always err on the side of caution. It is always better to look too conservative then too outlandish. Keep in mind there is nothing wrong with having your own style as long as that style is appropriate for the court you are in.

When I began to practice, several attorneys joked with me that I rarely wore a white dress shirt and tended to wear colored dress shirts. There is nothing wrong with colored dress shirts as they are still dress shirts, and I always wore a tie. If I had showed up in a bright colored tank top, that would have been a problem. You will have plenty of time to develop your own style, so be careful about people judging you on your clothing.

DEALING WITH OTHERS IN COURT

As already discussed, your reputation is key. Reputation determines how judges view you, how much the prosecutors listen to you, and how everyone treats you. When you are new, you don't have a reputation yet and you must constantly be careful to do the right things so that you can build a positive reputation and not a negative one.

Any experienced attorney will tell you that some of the most important people in the court are the bailiffs and clerks. The support people are not ruling on your motions, but make no mistake: they are incredibly powerful in their own way. Bailiffs and clerks determine when your matter is set, when the judge hears your case, and a lot of other matters that can simply your life or make it more difficult.

The difference between a bailiff liking an attorney or not liking them can mean the difference between the judge hearing your matter right away or in two weeks. A young attorney should be nice and courteous to the support staff simply because it is the right thing to do, and also because all the bailiffs and clerks talk. They not only talk to each other but they talk to their judges. You never want to be called into the judge's chambers and have the judge ask you why you think it's okay to be rude to his or her bailiff. Almost every week I see an attorney be rude or arrogant to a court support person, and it always amazes me that they are so actively sabotaging their careers. In addition to dealing with support staff, you will spend a lot of time dealing with prosecutors and opposing counsel.

Some attorneys think that if they yell and throw papers at the prosecutor or opposing counsel, this will be beneficial to their clients. I think some attorneys do it to put on a show for their clients. Some clients believe that if their attorney is being "aggressive", they are fighting hard for them. What always amazed me about this is that as a defense attorney, I am always trying to get something from the prosecutor. The prosecutor is the one that makes the offer to my client. If I am trying to get a better offer from a prosecutor, why would the prosecutor make me a better offer when I am yelling at them?

Prosecutors are people and they remember how attorneys treat them. I know that I can go up to any prosecutor that I have ever worked with and if I ask them for something they will at least consider it. They also know that if I am asking them something it will be for something reasonable. It is amazing how many defense attorneys I see being rude or condescending to prosecutors. There are several problems with this. The first problem is that we work with the same prosecutors a lot. Depending on the court, I may have close to a hundred cases a year with the same prosecutor. The second problem is when you are rude to prosecutors, this affects your reputation. Don't forget, reputation is everything.

The last person worth mentioning is the judge. They are easy to find as they usually have a black robe. There are a few simple rules for appearing before judges. Even if you do not like the judge personally, you must show respect to the court. Always stand when speaking to the judge. It is not improper to speak to a judge while sitting, but it is another way to show respect to the court. Never talk over the judge. When the judge is talking, you are not. Lastly, get to know your judge. Every judge has his or her own quirks. Some get furious if you chew gum; others get mad if you are one minute late. Other judges do not want you walking around the courtroom during trial. Always remember that it is THEIR courtroom and that they make the rules. Simple rules but ones many attorneys forget. There is one judge that holds my hand when talking to me. Do I think this is strange? Of course I do, but it's their courtroom, their rules.

ETHICS

Entire law school classes and many books are devoted to professional responsibility and ethics for lawyers. My goal here is to briefly give pointers to help young attorneys avoid ethical pitfalls. As a young attorney, there will be many ethics hazards that you will have to negotiate. Young attorneys have to deal with issues ranging from how to handle money, to client issues, to rules of court to rules of evidence.

One great resource available to young attorneys is experienced attorneys. When I was new I would call other attorneys almost every day with a ton of questions. I would ask questions about all kinds of stuff like how much to charge, how to handle a difficult client, and many other questions. Remember that more experienced attorneys have most likely had the issue that you are now facing. Most experienced attorneys do not mind you asking and actually like helping young attorneys. If one attorney doesn't know the answer to your question, try a different one.

Another good resource that is available to most attorneys is an ethics hotline that is run by the state bar. In Arizona, attorneys at the state bar that speak to attorneys and answer their questions staff the ethics hotline. These attorneys are very knowledgeable and helpful. When I was new to practicing, I once had a prosecutor subpoena me to court because I had a client who wanted out of his plea. I was not sure how much I could tell the court about what the client had told me before he entered the plea, so I called the hotline.

The hotline attorney was incredibly helpful and I felt a lot better after speaking to him. As a young attorney, you must always be careful to comply with the ethical rules in your state. The best way to do this is to actually know the rules. In Arizona, the rules are available online and can be easily accessed for reference. As you become more experienced, the rules will become second nature; but when you are new you will need to refer to them from time to time.

When I teach Professional Responsibility, I tell my students that on an exam, if they do not remember the specific rule they should pick the answer in which the attorney is honest and discloses everything and, often, that will be the correct answer. In practice, the same idea is true. Always err on the side of being too honest. Being too honest will never get you into trouble like lying will.

This seems simple, but many attorneys forget the importance of honesty. Just last week, I learned of an attorney that told his client not to come to court for a hearing. When the judge asked the defendant where his client was, the attorney lied. The attorney told the judge he did not know where the client was. The attorney ended up getting suspended from the practice of law when it was learned that he told his client not to show up.

There are a couple Model Rules that are worth discussing. Virtually every state has some version of the Model Rules. I am using the ABA model rule numbers. The specific numbering for your state may be different. There are a several rules that are worth discussing in some detail, such as Client–Lawyer Relationship Rule 1.1 Competence: A lawyer shall provide competent representation to a client. Competent representation requires the legal knowledge, skill, thoroughness, and preparation reasonably necessary for the representation. To a new attorney, this rule may be scary because it is hard to know what you are competent to handle.

A new attorney must be reasonable with himself or herself as to what they can honestly handle. A new attorney should not be afraid to take on a new type of case and learn along the way. While it is good to handle a new type of case, however, a new attorney must also not take on more than they can handle. If you are a criminal defense attorney and you do a lot of misdemeanor DUI work and you decide to take on a felony DUI even though it would be your first, this is reasonable. If you are a DUI attorney and you decide to take on a murder case, this would likely be a violation of rule 1.1. A new attorney must balance having enough work to pay the bills, learning by taking on new types of cases, and avoiding taking on work that he or she cannot handle.

Another set of rules that new attorneys must follow are the conflict rules. ABA Model Rules 1.6, 1.7, and 1.8 deal with conflicts. The rules should be read carefully and often. The rule of thumb is, if you think there is a conflict or a possible conflict, avoid the conflict. Some conflicts are obvious. Representing two sides that are litigating against each other is an obvious conflict. Some conflicts are not as obvious, and attorneys must be careful to look for them.

ABA Model Rule 7.1 deals with advertising. New attorneys must know that they can advertise but must follow specific rules. For example, in Arizona, an attorney's advertisement must feature several things. The ad must contain the name of at least one attorney in the firm, the firm's address, and the name of the firm. There are no rules that ads must be classy or professional, but a new attorney must always think of their reputation and how they will be perceived in the community. As a new attorney, do you want to thought of as the person with the tasteless, tacky ads?

Trial

A few quick words on trial. Often the attorney that is best prepared wins. A lot of people think trials are about showmanship and presentation. While those things can be important, being prepared is by far the most important thing. Being prepared means several things. You must know the facts of your case inside and out. I have seen many prosecutors that do not know the facts of their case. In many cities, the prosecutor is assigned the morning of the trial. As you will know your case and have had it for several months, this can give you an advantage. Being prepared also means you know the law. You know the statute, the positive case law, the negative law, and how various cases can affect your case.

Another part of being prepared is having your client ready. You have to know what your client is going to say. You must not only know what the client is going to say but how they are going to say it. I once lost a jury trial because my defendant got on the stand and said the video that the jury just watched never happened. The client must also know what to expect. They must know what the opposing counsel or the prosecutor is going to say, how long the trial will take, and who the witnesses are.

You as the attorney must remember that the whole process is new and scary for the client and plan accordingly. Think of a surgeon before an operation. The surgeon has probably done the procedure hundreds if not thousands of times, but the patient is still scared and worried. The patient is worried and scared because they have never had the surgery. Clients are the same way. The more the client knows what to expect, the more at ease they will be and the less they will bug you. The less your client is bugging you, the more you can focus on the trial.

Always remember to dress for trial. Be aware that you do not generally want to look flashy. Remember that the jury is evaluating how you are dressed, and if they don't like how you look, they can take that out on your jury. I have a defense attorney friend who once had a juror tell him that she convicted his client because she did not like the attorney's shoes. This is not rational, but jurors are people and you do not want to offend them. Always wear a jacket to trial. A lot of the time I will only wear a shirt and tie to court, but I will always wear a jacket to trial. If the prosecutor is wearing a jacket and you are not, the jury can think you are being disrespectful to the court.

The last important thing that new attorneys must remember is the value of brevity. What I mean by this is, if you can say something in a few words, don't use a few hundred words. Often new attorneys think that the longer they talk, the better it is for their case. In reality, often the person that can make a short, powerful statement is going to be better off. Juries and judges today have shorter attention spans than ever before. Attorneys must know this and prepare their arguments accordingly. Just as good writing should cut out everything that is not necessary, arguments in trial should do the same. Before trial, look at your written opening, cross, closing, and everything else, and ask what you can cut out.

Interviewing and Resumes

I first realized how bad most law students and recent law school grads were at interviewing when I began doing mock interviews at a local law school. The program is designed to help students get better at interviewing. I was amazed at how many of the students were not prepared to give a good interview. It doesn't matter if you own your own practice or hope to work for someone else; you will have to go through interviews. I think that since I have started my own practice, I have probably been through half a dozen interviews for various positions or contracts.

Interviewing, like everything else, takes practice and preparation. Some aspects of having a good interview are simple, and I don't need to spend a lot of time on them. You must be on time. This sounds simple, but I am always amazed when I see people coming in late to interviews. If you can't come on time to an interview, how will you come to work on time? If I am interviewing someone and they show up late, I know I will not hire them no matter how much I am impressed by them or how qualified they are.

Always remember that you must convince the person that is interviewing them how you will help them. Don't focus on how they can help you. Often I am at interviews where the person tells me that the job they are interviewing for would be a great opportunity and how excited they would be to work there. The person interviewing you doesn't care that they can help you. The person interviewing you cares how you can help them. Can you make their lives easier? Can you bring in clients? Can you show up on time and do good work? Always focus on what you bring to the table. You have to sell yourself. An employer wants to know that you are hard-working, motivated, and driven. As I have mentioned, I can teach someone to practice, but I can't teach someone to be motivated.

Another key aspect of interviewing is showing excitement for the work. Not the fake kind of excitement, but a real enthusiasm showing that you want to be working there. The person interviewing you can tell if you want the job or not. Also remember that you are likely not the only person being interviewed, and you must convince the employer why they should hire you and not someone else.

Before you ever get to an interview, you must have a resume. Your resume can't be good, very good, or any other variation of good. Your resume must be *perfect*. I have talked to countless employers that do not initially read resumes. They look at a resume to see if they like the layout and how the resume looks. If they do not like how the resume looks, they simply throw it away. The information in your resume could be amazing, but no one will read it if the resume gets thrown away because it doesn't look good. It is not uncommon for an employer to receive hundreds of resumes for one position. I know one government agency that recently received over 200 applications for one position. I also know of a local firm that was looking for a paralegal. That firm received over 400 resumes. Hopefully, you are beginning to understand why your resume must be perfect.

There are several things you can do to make your resume look better. Make sure that everything lines up. When you look at your resume, everything must be in place and neat. There are many examples of resumes online, if you need samples. Your resume should not be longer than one page. I have had many employers tell me that they do not like stapled resumes and will often not look at the second page. Many employers do not like resumes that are over one page because longer resumes create more volume. If an employer receives 400 resumes and each one is two pages, that's 800 pages of paper. Another reason your resume should be one page is because you should be able to fit everything important on a single page. No one cares if you played volleyball in high school or what clubs you were in in middle school. Your resume should start with college.

Like everything you write and will be turning in to someone, your resume must be proofread. The more people that proofread your resume, the better. An employer will glance at your resume for a split second and decide if they want to read it or not. If your resume looks anything less than perfect, they will throw it away. Prepare accordingly.

CONSTANT IMPROVEMENT AND BEING FLEXIBLE

As an attorney, you should always be working on improving your craft. It should not matter if you are in your first year of practice or your fiftieth; you should always be trying to improve. The constant goal of improving is a characteristic that all excellent attorneys have. It doesn't matter if the area of improvement is trial skills, client management, organization, or any other facet of practice. If you are not constantly working on getting better, you will never grow. Think of an athlete or performer. How good would an athlete be if she were not constantly working on getting better?

A lot of always getting better at your craft has to do with mindset. If you have a mindset that says, "I can get better at the following things," you will be more likely to improve. If you have a mindset that says, "I know as much as I need to know and I don't need to learn anything new," this will hold you back. It is important to tell yourself that no matter how skilled you are at something you can always improve. Even if the improvement is small, it is still an improvement.

Another important reason why you should always be trying to improve is that it will keep the work more interesting. If you are always doing the same thing at the same level, you will get bored. One of the best things about the legal profession is that there is always room for growth. It doesn't matter what type of law you practice; there is always something new to learn. There is always a new way to organize your office, a new way to do a trial opening, or a new way to reassure a nervous client. An important part of always improving is staying flexible.

A good attorney must be flexible in how they do things. If someone has a way of doing something that is better than how you do it, why not adopt the new method? If you have always done jury closing one way but someone tells you about a method that is likely to be more effective, why not try it? Often attorneys will be inflexible and not willing to try different approaches. Once I was talking to a prosecutor about how she was marking files. I told her that the way she was doing it was hard to read and confusing, and I suggested a different way that would be easier for her and for me. She told me that she had always done it the other way and would not change.

Today, after having thousands of clients, I still talk to other attorneys and ask for their advice and suggestions on how I can improve. Just last week I was at a party with an excellent defense attorney who suggested I change one part of how I talk to clients. Instead of being defensive and telling her that my method was fine, I listened to her and thought about what she said. I realized that she was correct, and I have since adopted her suggestion in how I speak to clients. As an attorney, you will have people suggest things to you all the time. Not all of the suggestions will be good, but you should always keep an open mind to doing something differently.

CHAPTER 9
DEALING WITH CLIENTS AND ATTORNEYS

A large part of any attorney's day is dealing with either clients or other attorneys. The other attorneys may be people in your office, prosecutors, opposing counsel, or co-counsel. Being skillful in dealing with clients and other attorneys can be the difference between enjoying your work and hating it. An attorney who is good at dealing with others is easy to see. The opposite type of attorney is equally easy to see. Young attorneys often expect that clients may be difficult but are surprised at how difficult other attorneys can be. My goal is to help young attorneys not only deal better with difficult clients but difficult attorneys as well.

The best and the worst part of being an attorney can be dealing with clients. There are few feelings better than when a client tells you what an amazing job you did and gives you a hug. There are fewer worse feelings than when a client tells you he is filing a bar complaint for some perceived injustice. Every attorney has stories of clients that have loved them and clients that have hated them. Lawyers provide a service to clients. Our goal is to make clients happy, but new attorneys must be realistic in that some clients will never be happy and nothing can be done about it. Sometimes it really is them and not you.

CLIENTS AND SETTING PRICES

One area where new attorneys (including me) have a hard time is in dealing with clients and money. How much money to charge, when to collect money, when to sue a client, how to bill clients, and dealing with clients who are unhappy about how much they owe are difficult issues. One area that is important to a healthy practice is setting prices. When I started, I had a hard time setting prices because I had a bad habit of underquoting clients. If you underquote by a little bit, it is no big deal, but if you underquote by a lot, it can be a large problem. After an attorney has been practicing for a while, it is easy to know how much to charge. Before you figure out how much to charge, you need to figure out if you will be charging a flat fee or an hourly fee. Your field of law will often dictate how you charge.

Some fields of law such as criminal law or estate planning are a lot more accustomed to flat fees. A flat fee is exactly what it sounds like. A client comes to you and says I want to hire you. You tell the client how much you will charge to handle the entire case. An hourly fee is the opposite, and the attorney charges for each hour worked. If you are doing civil work, there is a good chance you will be billing hourly. If you are not sure if you should bill hourly or bill a flat fee, talk to other attorneys in the area and they will know. Other attorneys are also a great resource for help with setting fees. Even today, when a client wants to hire me for a type of case I have not handled before, I will call one of my attorney friends who has handled that type of case and ask what they charge.

It is also important to get as much information from your potential client as possible before quoting them a price. I learned this lesson the hard way. I had a client call me and tell me he had a drug possession case. I falsely assumed he would be eligible for probation and told him I would do the case for $1500. This was my first mistake.

Generally, you should not quote prices over the phone. Have the person come to your office and talk face to face. One attorney with over thirty years' experience told me he always has potential clients come to the office and gives them his "eyebrow test." He explained to me that if their eyebrows go up when he tells them the price (showing they are shocked at how much he wants to charge), he lowers the price. Remember, you can always adjust your price down from your original quote but not the opposite. If you ask a client for $5000 and they say no problem, you can't then say well what about $6000.

After my potential client came in and hired me, he told me he had multiple felony prior convictions and was on felony probation for a felony less than two years ago. After doing a little research, I figured out that he was looking at close to 20 years in prison. The mistake was entirely my own, and I learned from it. I now have a checklist of questions that I ask potential clients. If they do not want to answer the questions, this is a huge red flag and I do not want their business because they will be trouble down the road. Like with many other things, a little information up front can save a lot of trouble down the road. These are some of the questions I now ask all potential clients:

- Have you ever been charged with a crime before?
- Have you ever been convicted of a crime?
- Any felony or misdemeanor convictions?
- Are you on probation or parole?
- What court is this charge out of?
- How many total counts are you being charged with?
- Have you been to court on this charge yet?
- Will any motions be necessary?
- Have you spoken to other attorneys?
- Have you gotten price quotes from other attorneys?

CLIENTS, GETTING MONEY UP FRONT, AND COLLECTING MONEY OWED

You must get at least some money up front. Unless you have a client that you trust and know will pay, you must get some kind of money up front. Getting money up front is important for several reasons. The first is that it shows you that, the client is serious about hiring you. It is very different when a client says they want to hire you and when they actually pay you. The second reason it is important to get money up front is because the client does not really appreciate your work until they have given you money. Ask any attorney and they will tell you that they have heard every excuse possible as to why the client cannot pay them up front and that if you start their case for free they will pay you soon. The following is only a partial list of reasons clients have told me they do not have money but will soon:

- Injury settlement money is coming in
- Money from a will or trust is coming to them
- Awaiting income tax return
- Parents will lend them the money
- Divorce settlement
- Payday is next week
- New business is taking off and will soon pay off
- Disability payment is in the mail
- Etc. . .

How much money you get up front will depend on several variables. In criminal defense work we try to get as much money up front as we can. We know that often the money we get up front will be the only money we get. If you know this as an attorney, this is not a problem, but if you think the client will pay more and they don't, then it's a problem. The reason we know that often the money we get up front will be the only money we ever see is because many of our clients are less than honest. Many of our clients are, in fact, criminals.

FEE AGREEMENTS

You *must* have a written fee agreement. There are no exceptions. Many conflicts between attorneys and their clients could have been avoided if there had been a clear fee agreement. The fee agreement is necessary because it spells out what the attorney will and will not do and for how much. The fee agreement must be clear about whether the fee is a flat fee or an hourly fee and should specify how and when the payment will be made. Most state bar websites will have a sample fee agreement. When you are starting out, it is not a bad idea to use the template.

It is important that you review the agreement with the client to make sure they clearly understand what they are and are not hiring you for before they sign the fee agreement. It is also important that your fee agreement states whether or not it covers a trial. Some attorneys have a flat fee for the pretrial and trial parts of the case. Some attorneys have one fee for all of the pretrial work and a separate fee for the trial. Obviously, if a client thinks they are paying for everything but you plan on charging them a separate trial fee, they will not be happy. A fee agreement should also state whether experts are necessary and approximately how much those experts can cost. I do a lot of DUI work, and I have in my fee agreement a sentence saying that if the client wants an expert or the case requires an expert at trial, there will be an extra fee, and the expert normally charges about $600 for the court appearance.

No matter how simple of a matter you are handling, you must have a fee agreement. I recently handled a very simple matter for a client. They had old fines they owed to the court, and they paid me to go to court with them to ask a judge to get rid of some of the fines. I went to court and asked, and the judge said no. I thought that I had done everything that we had agreed to, but the client though otherwise. He thought that I would make as many court appearances as he wanted. The mistake was mine, as I did not have a fee agreement. If I had had one, I could have avoided the confusion.

CLIENT MANAGEMENT

One of the best ways to manage clients and keep clients from complaining and causing problems for you is to manage their expectations. I have a friend who is a criminal defense attorney. He has been practicing law longer then I have been alive. He told me that when a client comes into his office, he always tells them they are going to prison for a long, long time.

After the client freaks out, he says he will try to get them a reduced sentence. This is a very important lesson for all new attorneys. If you tell your client that they are facing a 10 on the disaster scale and the end result is a 7, they will be relatively happy. If you tell the client that they are facing a 2 on the disaster scale and the end result is a 4, they will think you didn't do a very good job and should have done more. It sounds strange, but I promise you this is true, and you will see it for yourself.

Often, new attorneys have a hard time with managing client expectations because they do not want to give the client bad news. You should not exaggerate the possible outcome, but you should also be sure not to make the situation sound better than it actually is. Managing expectations is not only important for criminal defense attorneys, but for all attorneys. Managing expectations is about more than just the outcome of the case.

Managing expectations also has to do with what the attorney expects of you. If you don't want the client to think that he can call you ten times a day, late at night, and on the weekends, you must be clear with him when you are available and when you are not. I know many attorneys that give out their cell phone numbers to clients. Many attorneys do not give out their cell phone numbers and tell their clients to call the office. Either approach is okay, as long as the client knows what to expect.

Managing expectations is important from the first time you meet a prospective client. Setting the tone of the client–attorney relationship is just as important. The client must know that you are in charge and cannot be pushed around. Many clients will try to take advantage of an inexperienced attorney and tell her what to do and how to do it. You must always remember that you are the attorney and that the client came to you.

A client is always watching the attorney and deciding if the attorney knows what he is doing and if it would be wise to listen to him. If a client sees that you are in charge and in control, the client is more likely to listen and your life will be easier. The opposite is also true. If a client senses that you are insecure in your work, the client will take advantage of this and start to take charge.

Clients generally do not understand whether or not you are doing quality work, but they watch for things they do understand. I often tell students that how you say something is more important than what you say when speaking to a client. When you are explaining a complex legal theory to a client, the client will likely not understand. What the client will understand is your tone. Think of your dog or cat. A dog does not understand words, but it understands tone. A dog understands when someone speaking to it is confident, scared, or indecisive. Clients are often the same way.

Clients will listen for tone, but they will also watch your actions. Clients notice things like whether or not you are on time. Clients notice if your paperwork is ready when you come to court or if are you a disheveled mess. Clients notice how you carry yourself with opposing counsel, with the prosecutor, or with the judge. I know many attorneys that are not very good at knowing the law but make a great presentation for their clients, and the clients think they are the best attorneys in the world.

Not all clients are the same, and there are several types that you will see over and over. One type of client you will encounter is a client that has never been to a lawyer. This type of client is common in any field of law. This type of client will often have a million questions and will require some hand holding. I say hand holding figuratively, but sometimes it will be literal. I once had a senior citizen female client that would grab on to my hand when walking into court. An attorney has to remember that many people have never met an attorney. Attorneys tend to forget this because it is our profession and we know many attorneys.

To many clients, meeting an attorney is intimidating, and you must work to make the client comfortable. This type of client will often bring a small, or not so small, support system. I have seen clients bring their entire families to court for support. There is no problem with bringing people to court with them, but if they are coming to your office, you want to be clear with them how having people there affects the attorney–client privilege.

Clients that have never used an attorney before are generally easier to manage then the next type of client.

Frequent flier clients are present in every field of law. In civil practice, they may be always trying to sue current or former business partners. In the criminal world, they are clients that are always getting in trouble for one thing or another. The advantage of frequent flier clients is that they generally know what to expect. They have been to court before and know what to expect in court. These types of clients also know how much legal services cost. If the client has hired you before, you will have a working relationship, which will make the handing of their case easier.

The downside of frequent flier clients is that they often think they know more than you. They may try telling you what to do and often think that their legal experience entitles them to an honorary law degree. Every client is different, and there are no blanket rules, but frequent flier clients are generally pushier than clients that have never used an attorney before. With frequent flier clients, it is crucial that you establish that you are in charge.

I once had a client who was charged with a DUI. This was his second or third DUI, and he thought he knew the law. The problem with his case was that he hit a parked police cruiser while the officer was watching him. Needless to say, the client was very drunk as he drove into the police car. The client was trying to tell me that the officer had to have probable cause to stop him, and he had none, and the case should be thrown out. There is nothing more dangerous than a client who thinks he knows the law.

Another type of client that you will have is the habitual liar. They will lie about anything and everything and not think twice about it. I have had these clients, and I can be watching a video of them shoplifting and they will sit in front of me and tell me that they were not shoplifting. When I remind them that we are watching a video showing them shoplifting, they will tell me that it is not them.

With habitual liar clients, is important that you not believe anything they tell you. You must verify everything. The good thing about these clients is that they lie so much that it is usually fairly easy to catch on and act accordingly. If you figure out that they are lying about everything before they hire you, you may not want their business. If the client will be more of a headache than they are worth, you may not want them to hire you.

Just several days ago, I had a trial with a client that was a frequent flier and a habitual liar. He was in his mid-forties and had been to prison several times. In his current case, he went over to his neighbor's and started peeing on his front door. When the neighbor opened the door, my drunk defendant attacked the neighbor. At the trial, three officers testified that my client was incredibly drunk, and all three officers saw a bottle of vodka in his hands. The neighbor also testified and said he knew the defendant well from other incidents in the complex and he clearly recognized my client. My client testified and said he never drinks alcohol, was not drinking on the night in question, and didn't pee on anyone's door. After he was convicted, he started yelling that he wanted an appeal.

The last type of client worth mentioning is the client that is mad at the world. They can be any age and think nothing is their fault and that the world is out to get them. These types of clients are almost never happy and they are virtually impossible to make happy. If they are going to hire you, you need to know from the start that they are not likely to end up happy. No matter the type of law you practice, you will have clients that are mad at the world. You can usually see these clients from a mile away. They will complain about everything and blame everyone.

An attorney must always be in charge, and with this type of client it is crucial that the attorney make it clear that they are in charge. This type of client will blame you for everything that they can. This is what they do. Clients that are mad at the world are usually jaded about everything, and their attitude reflects their outlook. Ultimately, no matter the type of client you have, you must build trust with them. No matter if your client is crazy, a liar, aggressive, or perfectly normal, your life will be a lot easier and the representation will go much smoother if the client trusts you.

Trust must be built. Clients want to know that you as their attorney tried for them and fought for them. A lot of my criminal defense court-appointed clients have never had anyone in a suit fight for them. When they see an attorney fighting for them and doing everything they can to help them, they will be grateful. With any relationship, trust is hard to build and easy to lose. If you tell a client that you will call them on a certain day, you must call them on that day. If you promise something to your client, you must deliver on that promise. If you break a promise to a client, they will not only remember it, but they will tell other people how their attorney let them down. This is not only bad for your own reputation but also for the reputation of attorneys in general. An attorney must never forget that a client trusts them to handle something very important to the client. Whether it be a criminal case, a divorce, a lawsuit, or any other legal matter, that matter is of great importance to the client.

I recently had an Ethiopian client who was charged with a DUI. At first, he was not very trusting and told me that back home, most attorneys and police were corrupt and that no one had ever really fought for him. He was a court-appointed client, so he falsely assumed that I would not try very hard for him. He assumed he would be found guilty, but I told him I would do everything I could for him.

After a multiple-day jury trial, the jury was deadlocked and the judge declared a mistrial. After the prosecutor refiled the charges, we had a second jury trial. After another multiple-day trial, the jury was out for hours but came back with a guilty verdict. The client was not very upset about the verdict, but told me that I had done more for him they he ever thought an attorney would do. This is how attorneys build trust with clients.

DEALING WITH DIFFICULT CLIENTS

You will have difficult clients. This is a reality and every attorney will tell you they have difficult clients. There are several things a new attorney must understand about some difficult clients. Many difficult clients will never be happy and new attorneys must understand that. No matter how hard their attorney tries for them, they will never be happy. New attorneys must understand that often when the client is unhappy it is not about what the attorney did but about other things in the difficult client's life. Difficult clients will often not listen at all. They will put blame everywhere they can but never on themselves.

I once had a client who was charged with pointing a gun at a small child out his apartment window. We had a trial and many witnesses testified they saw my client point the gun out of his window. All the witnesses were credible and all told the exact same story. As expected, my client was convicted and, as expected, he took no responsibility for his actions. After the trial he told me that maybe if I had done a better job he would not have been found guilty. This is a typical difficult client.

Another client I recently had also demonstrates how difficult clients typically behave. I knew the client was going to be difficult before I ever met him. He had been reassigned to me from a different attorney. That attorney had withdrawn because the client kept calling his office and kept yelling at the entire staff. The client was in his late seventies and was arrested for telling the people at the food stamp office that he was going to kill everyone there. He was mad because his food stamp benefits had been reduced. When I met with him, he told me he wanted a trial and that he was innocent. I told him that they had him on video threating to kill people. He told me that did not prove anything. I told him it proved the charge he was charged with. Eventually I got him no jail and he pled guilty, but he always maintained he did nothing wrong. No matter how difficult a client is, an attorney must always remain professional.

CLIENTS WITH MENTAL HEALTH ISSUES

No matter what type of law you practice, you will have clients with mental health issues. Many people think it is only the criminal defense clients who have mental health issues, but this is not true. Attorneys in family law, estate planning, and civil work will all have clients with mental health issues. Mental health issues can be anything from dementia or Alzheimer's to Schizophrenia or any other number of conditions.

There are several things to keep in mind when dealing with clients with mental health issues. The first thing to remember is that you, as the attorney, must be extra patient. A client with mental health issues may need you to speak slower or to explain things several times. Be accommodating and try to make the client feel like you are being accommodating without talking down to them.

One final important thing to remember when dealing with clients with mental health issues is that they often have support people that may be helpful to you. By support people I mean family members, doctors, caseworkers, physiologists, and anyone else that may be able to help. Often the client will tell you about the people helping them, but other times you will have to find them on your own. Generally, when I have a client with mental health issues, I will ask them if they have a caseworker. The caseworker can often give me more information so that I can better assist the client. Always remember that even when dealing with clients with mental health issues there are confidentiality and privilege issues.

NOT JUDGING YOUR CLIENTS

An attorney must always remember not to judge their clients. Often clients are embarrassed or scared when talking to an attorney and you must always be aware of this. A good attorney must try to make their client more comfortable.

A young attorney who is no longer doing defense work once met with a client and did something a defense attorney should never do. After the client told them what happened, the attorney told them what they did was stupid. It should be clear why this person is no longer practicing defense work.

I once represented a young lady who was charged with a DUI. There is nothing unusual about someone being charged with a DUI. The unusual thing about her case was that she was so drunk she called the police on herself. The woman had not only called the police on herself for drunk driving, she did so while naked in her car. At the time the police showed up, she was parked in the middle of the intersection totally naked. When the police arrested her and put her in the back of the police car she peed herself. When I was talking to her she was obviously very embarrassed. Part of being a professional is to make clients feel comfortable and not to embarrass them any further. Even though it can be difficult, you have to refrain from making judgmental comments to protect to the client's feelings. Another one of my memorable clients was arrested for assault after slapping her husband. What was memorable about this case was that she slapped him during group sex gone wrong. My defendant and her husband met another couple at a hotel and went to a room to have group sex. As my defendant's husband was having sex with the other woman, the condom broke. The husband told his wife not to worry as he had had a vasectomy. The other woman chimed in that she had had a hysterectomy. At this point my defendant freaked out and slapped her husband, who quickly called the police on his own wife.

I can't tell you how hard it is to keep a straight face when reading such a police report. I remember thinking about what the police were thinking when they showed up to the hotel and found four naked people in a hotel room. While I was reading the police report to the woman, she was obviously horribly embarrassed. Imagine how horrified and embarrassed she would have been if I said "Wow, what were you thinking?" I did not say anything to her not related to the case and as we talked she saw I was being professional; over time, she calmed down and felt more comfortable.

TOO MUCH EMPATHY VS. NOT CARING AT ALL

A good attorney has to be able to balance having empathy for their clients with protecting their own emotions. There are attorneys that go too far on both extremes. There are attorneys that are completely consumed with their clients and their needs. They take on all the emotions of their clients' cases and, over time, they become burned out. A typical defense attorney will hear hundreds, if not thousands, of sad, heart breaking stories every year. If that attorney takes on all that sadness as their own, it can be difficult to deal with.

The other extreme are the attorneys who do not care at all. A client will tell them that they just had a child die and the attorney will say that is not my problem. These attorneys do a great deal of harm to their clients as the clients are often looking for someone to listen to them. That attorney pushes the client away when the client needs them.

The key is balance. There is no secret to balancing empathy with not caring at all. Many attorneys go their whole career without ever learning how to do it. Most attorneys learn to balance the two with time. When I started, I was closer to the caring too much end of the spectrum. I have learned to protect myself emotionally while still caring and listening to clients.

A good attorney must always remember that the client is there because they need your help. Most times that an attorney has a client sitting in front of them, it is one of the lowest points of the client's life. The client might be facing jail, divorce, a lawsuit, a bankruptcy, business trouble, or other problems. You must protect yourself emotionally but not become completely cold to your clients.

DEALING WITH DIFFICULT ATTORNEYS

> "If it doesn't make you money or make you happy, don't do it" –A. Carolla-

Just as I can assure you that will have difficult clients, I can assure you that you will have to deal with difficult attorneys. They may be opposing counsel, prosecutors, or other attorneys in your field. There are a million reasons why attorneys are difficult to other attorneys. Some are naturally that way. Some are burnt out and angry at the world. Some will be difficult to other attorneys as a strategy (not a very good strategy, but still a strategy).

I have had to deal with many difficult attorneys, but one stands out. I got a call from the court asking me if I could cover for another attorney. The person who was supposed to cover had double booked and the court needed my help. The court told me to bill the attorney, so I did. After not paying me for close to a month, the attorney told me I was charging him too much. I told him I was charging my regular rate and was not charging him anything extra. The attorney then sent me a letter that he would not be using me for coverage anymore and that he was telling other attorneys not to hire me. I wanted to respond, but I chose to take the high road.

Some attorneys will be difficult to deal with directly. I have seen attorneys throw papers at prosecutors, yell at prosecutors, and have outbursts in court. Some attorneys will be difficult in weird passive aggressive ways, like writing nasty emails or by not paying for your work on time. You cannot control how other attorneys behave, but you can control how you react. I have had to deal with several unprofessional and difficult attorneys and I have always tried to take the high road. I have wanted to write back emails and call people names and confront people, but I always remembered the great American philosopher Adam Carolla, who once said something that I have thought about often and shared with a lot of people. He said that every time he deals with someone difficult and wants to retaliate and respond, he asks himself if his response will make him happy or make him money. If the answer is no, then don't do it. Sounds simple, but like everything, it takes practice.

CHAPTER 10
MANAGING YOUR PRACTICE

MANAGING YOUR MONEY

How you manage money will determine if your practice survives or fails. It doesn't matter how good your reputation is, how many cases you win, or how much clients like you if you are out of money. It always amazes me how many attorneys are terrible at managing money. Some attorneys are excellent at making money, but because they do not know how to manage it, they run into problems.

From buying expensive cars to expensive toys to trips, attorneys are excellent at blowing money. Many attorneys get into trouble with money in the same way as many professional athletes. If an attorney gets a new car, the other attorney in his office may want to get an even more expensive car to show off and to compete with the attorney. If one attorney has two homes, someone else will want three. One good way to manage your money is to keep track of where it goes and how much you are actually making.

One good way to manage money is to use good accounting software. I have always used QuickBooks Online and would recommend it to new attorneys. The program is simple to use and does a great job of tracking who owes you money and your spending patterns. It doesn't matter if you use QuickBooks or another program, but you must keep track of your expenses. I can easily check to see how much I spent on my car last year or last month, how much money I spent on eating out, or the cost of my month utilities. A business cannot control expenses if it doesn't know what those expenses are.

Another great feature about QuickBooks is that I can easily see who owes me money and if I owe anyone money. Not only will the program tell me who owes me money, it will tell me how late they are in paying. I can organize outstanding invoices by date so I know who I need to worry about getting paid from and whose invoice is the oldest. I have been using QuickBooks for four years and I am still discovering cool features that I did not know about.

At the end of every day, I input receipts. Since the program is online, at the end of the year, all my CPA has to do in log on to my account with the temporary password that I give him and prepare my taxes. The program being online is convenient for more than just end-of-year tax purposes. If I ever have a question about one of my accounts or want my CPA to look at something, all he has to do is log on. I am always amazed how many attorneys still have a shoebox full of receipts that they take to their CPA at the end of the year. Actually, I am amazed how many attorneys don't have a CPA.

This brings me to the next important aspect of managing money. Get a good CPA. With CPAs, like with all professionals, you get what you pay for. If your CPA charges ten bucks an hour, but works out of his car, you are likely to go to prison for tax evasion. My CPA is not cheap, but I know he does good work. For me, paying him well is worth it because I know that my taxes will be done correctly and if there is ever a problem he will be there to help. I knew nothing about taxes when I started, so I knew that it would be important to have a professional helping me.

I am often amazed at how many attorneys do not have separate accounts for their business and their personal accounts. You should be very careful to keep your personal accounts separate from your business accounts. Do not use a personal credit card for business purchases. Do not use business checks to pay for personal expenses. Make sure that your online personal bank account is not linked to your business bank account. If you have a personal credit card and a business credit card, make sure they are different colors so you don't use the wrong one by accident. Also, make sure your personal and business checks are different colors.

Another good way to manage money is to not spend a lot of it. A lot of young attorneys fail at having their own practice not because they are bad attorneys but because their spending is greater than their income. This problem is not unique to new attorneys. I know attorneys that make huge amounts of money but manage to spend even more, and as a result they are still broke. If you make a half a million dollars a year but spend a half million dollars plus one dollar, you are still broke.

Many attorneys are drawn to expensive offices, expensive cars, and an expensive lifestyle. Often this is a quick way to go broke. A good example is a car payment. If your payments are $300 a month instead of $600 a month, that's an extra $3,600 in your pocket over a year. Over five years, the savings are $18,000. Now for the real savings: If you don't have a car payment at all, that's an extra $18,000 dollars in your pocket. Do you want a new car or an extra $18,000?

Little expenses can add up, too. Instead of eating out for lunch every day, consider bringing a bag lunch. If an attorney eats out every day, it will cost approximately $200 a month. Over a year, the total is $2,400, and over five years the total climbs $12,000. The lesson is simple; if you bring lunch from home, you will save $12,000 dollars. Obviously, you will eat out sometimes, but think of how much money you will save. I know many attorneys that eat out every day and I often think of how much those lunches are costing them.

Try to save money in every place possible. Think of things like your gas mileage. If you drive a lot, having a car with excellent gas mileage can make a big difference. Last year, I drove over 21,000 miles in between different courts. If I drove a car that got terrible gas mileage, I would have paid thousands of dollars more for gas than I had to. The point is not that you have to sell your car and buy a hybrid, but that you must be creative in trying to save money.

One other place where you may be able to save money is by having a cell phone instead of a landline. A traditional office line setup can cost hundreds of dollars a month. A simple cell phone can be purchased for a couple of bucks, and you can get unlimited minutes for about twenty dollars a month. Remember, when a client calls you, they don't know if you have a fancy office setup or a cheap cell phone. A cell phone also has the added benefit or being portable.

Another important part of managing your money is deciding what forms of payment you will accept. I always require that new clients either pay by cash, a money order, or a cashier's check. If you know or trust the client, a check can be acceptable. Be careful with checks, as they are often bad and will bounce. I once had a client charged with felony check fraud try to pay me with a check. Credit cards can be a convenient option for clients, as clients often do not have enough money in their bank accounts to pay.

There are several things to watch out for if you accept credit cards. First, be careful what the credit card company or the bank is charging you in fees. Normally, you should expect to pay somewhere around two to three percent per transaction. Watch out for hidden bank fees and transaction fees that may be buried in small print in your bank statement. The second thing to watch out for with credit cards is the challenge period. A person paying with a credit card has a certain amount of time to challenge the transaction. This is important to you because after a client pays you, they can challenge the transaction and the credit card company can put a hold on the transaction or ask for the money back. The bottom line with credit cards is to be careful.

The last and perhaps most important aspect of managing money is to have cash saved up. The more cash you have on hand, the more comfortable you will feel. When you have a big payday from a client or a settlement, hold on to as much of that money as possible. If you have a slow month, having cash saved up can be the difference between your practice surviving or closing.

INSURANCE

An important part of managing your practice is having adequate insurance. There are several types of insurance that you need to have. You must have malpractice insurance. I'm not saying that you *should* have malpractice insurance; you *MUST* have malpractice insurance. Malpractice insurance is one of those things that you hope you never need, but when you do need it, it can save your practice. A surprising number of attorneys do not have malpractice insurance as a cost cutting measure. I once spoke to an attorney that chose not to have malpractice insurance so he could afford a fancier office. At first I thought he was joking; he was not.

How much you pay for malpractice insurance will depend on several factors. The first is how long you have been practicing. Insurance providers figure that the longer you have been practicing, the more clients you will have had. The more clients you have had, the more likely that one of them will sue you. Malpractice insurance usually gets more expensive every year. The increase in price is gradual but continues. The second factor that will determine how much you pay is the type of law you practice.

Attorneys in different areas of law are charged different amounts. The reason is that attorneys in certain types of law are more likely to have claims for money brought against them. If a criminal defense attorney screws up, a client's case may be overturned. The client is not likely to win money, so the insurance company won't have to pay anything. If a personal injury attorney screws up, the insurance company can be out a lot of money.

For example, if a personal injury attorney misses the statute of limitations on a client's case and the client sues for malpractice, the insurance company will be writing a check. Since a personal injury attorney is more likely to cost the insurance company more money, they are charged more. When I first began to look for malpractice insurance, I was told that criminal defense attorneys have some of the lowest premiums while personal injury attorneys have the highest.

Make sure you shop around for the best price. This was one of the many lessons I learned the hard way. My first year in practice, I went with a provider that I saw advertised in the Arizona State Bar Magazine. The price sounded reasonable, so I went with them. I did not shop around and just accepted the price. When it was time to renew, I shopped around and found the same policy for $200 less. Remember, every penny counts. Also, keep in mind that the first couple of years you will not have a lot of clients, so you are less likely to need the insurance. Get a sufficient amount of coverage, but you will not likely need millions of dollars of coverage. Obviously, the more coverage, the more you will pay in premiums.

Malpractice insurance is a good start, but not the only type of insurance you should have. You need to have health insurance. The reason is simple. If you get sick or need surgery, the cost could wipe you out. One surgery could cost hundreds of thousands of dollars. I would recommend a very basic policy. Most of the policies have the word "catastrophic" or "emergency" coverage (comforting, I know). The good thing about health insurance is that if you are relatively young and healthy, a basic policy will not cost very much. Like with everything else, remember to shop around. The difference in price between two similar policies can be huge.

Finally, there is a third type of insurance to consider. Many young attorneys do not have disability insurance, but they should. If you don't know what disability insurance is, think of the Aflack duck. If you are not able to work, the policy pays you a preset amount for a preset amount of time. The reason young attorneys should consider this type of insurance is because when you are a solo, everything is on you. If you are not able to work, you will have to hire someone to go to court. You will also need a way to pay the bills. If I am not working, I am not making money. The chances of something happening to you so you are not able to work are low, but this does not mean you should not plan for it. The good thing about disability insurance is that it is very cheap. A reasonable policy can be bought for $30 to $40 a month. A good way to learn about any type of insurance is to speak with a broker that can answer all of your questions about different types of policies.

FILES

Keeping good files is essential. Keeping a good file is not difficult, but many attorneys do not do it. I am always amazed when I see some attorney pull a wad of papers out of their suitcase and try to figure out what paper is what. There are a million different systems for filing, and I'm not sure there is a correct one or a wrong one. Some people will keep their files in an alphabetical order, others by chronological order. Some people will design their own system with code letters and code numbers. Whatever system you use, be consistent and start using the system right away. When you only have three clients, keeping track of their files will not be difficult. But once you have 300 or 3,000 files, you will have to find the correct files while you are running out the door, late to court.

Keeping a neat, updated file is just as important as a good file organization system. A long time ago when I was interning at the Washtenaw County Public Defender's Office in Ann Arbor, Michigan, I had a boss there that had a rule that I still follow. He told us that anytime we picked up a file, we should note what we did with it. He told us that if we were hit by a bus, another attorney should be able to pick up the file and know everything that had been done up to that point. I will give you the same advice. Every time you pick up a file for any reason, note what you did in the file. You don't have to go into great length, but make a note.

If you look through the file, call the client, prepare a motion—anytime you do anything—make a note. This is an important practice for several reasons. The first reason is that, unavoidably, you will have a client who tries to throw you under the bus and complain to someone that you have not done any work. The unhappy client will complain to a judge or the state bar. This is the time you will be glad that you kept a good file.

I once had a client that was the classic difficult client. Nothing was ever her fault, and everyone else was to blame. She had received over twenty speeding tickets in less than two years and now had a reckless driving and criminal speeding charge. She drew the attention of the officers following her as she was going in excess of eighty miles an hour, weaving in and out of traffic while applying makeup with both hands. She had gotten so many speeding tickets in one area that when the officer pulled her over, he recognized her from when he had cited her two weeks ago.

I told her we did not have a good case for trial as the police had recorded the entire sequence of events and the video clearly showed her not only speeding, but driving dangerously. She was not happy with what I had to say, so she approached the judge and told her she wanted a different defense attorney, stating I had done nothing for her and had not returned her phone calls. Fortunately for me, I had kept a good record in the file. I read to the judge all the dates I had met with this client, all the times I had called her, all the times I had emailed her, and all other dates I had worked on her case. When I was done, the judge turned to the defendant and said, "It seems like Mr. Benikov has done quite a bit for you." The defendant never complained about me again.

Properly closing out a file is just as important as keeping an organized file. When you are done with a client and their case is concluded, you need to have a system for closing out their file. The system can be as simple as looking through the file and making sure everything has been done correctly. Some attorneys mail the client a letter telling them that the representation in the matter has ended. This is a good idea, so that the client clearly understands that attorney is no longer representing them.

Once you close out the file, you must keep it for a certain amount of time. Different states have different rules for how long attorneys must keep closed files. Make sure you know what the rules are in your state and that you comply. Once the proper amount of time has gone by, you can throw the file out, but make sure that everything is properly shredded.

LETTERHEAD, BUSINESS CARDS, AND WEBSITES

The reason I have letterhead, business cards, and websites in one section is because they are all a reflection of your practice. Often, before a client meets you in person, they will see your business card or your website. A good business card is kind of like good service at a restaurant. When the service is good, most people don't notice; but when the service is bad, it is very obvious. I have seen a lot of bad attorney business cards. I have seen ones that look like they should belong to a clown doing kids' birthday parties. I have seen cards without an address. When I see a card without an address, I assume the attorney is working out of their car. I have seen business cards with a cartoon font or text that is illegible. When picking out a card, there are a few things to consider.

The font has to be big enough to be clearly seen. If you are doing estate planning or any field where your clients are going to be older, you will want a larger font. The font will often look bigger on the computer than it will on the actual card. You will want to get a sample of the card to see how the font will look when printed. I learned this the hard way when I got my first cards made. When the printer and I designed them, they looked like a good size, but when they were delivered to me, the contact information was way too small and hard to read.

Something else to keep in mind with cards is that you get what you pay for. If you go online and do one of those free card deals, you will get your money's worth. Good cards will cost more, but they will look better. A decent printer will give you cards that are sturdy, have nice ink, and look presentable.

One other thing to think about with cards is a logo. One of the most common logos for attorneys is a scale. When I designed my first cards, I specifically did not use a scale. I thought they were passé and only something old attorneys used. I have kind of come around on scales. They are an easy way for people to know you are an attorney. Remember, many people do not know a lot about attorneys, but everyone knows a scale means you are an attorney. One idea to consider is to design your own scale. With your own design, you still get a scale, but it will look different than everyone else's. Remember, your cards are a reflection of you and you want to make the best impression possible. Same thing goes for letterhead.

You want letterhead that makes a good impression. You want letterhead that says it belongs to an attorney that is doing well (even if you are not). Whether attorneys like it or not, presentation is a large part of our business. The quality of letterhead and business cards will be partially determined by the clients you are trying to attract. If most of your clients are court-appointed and/or low income, they don't care what your letterhead looks like. Most of them will not know what letterhead is and don't care to know. On the other hand, if you are trying to attract wealthy clients or business professionals, they will expect quality letterhead and business cards. Also, it is important that your letterhead and business cards match.

One last thing worth thinking about when it comes to letterhead is having your own greeting cards. Having personalized greeting cards to say thank you or to wish people happy holidays can be a great tool for generating business. People remember actual cards they receive a lot more than an email. When another attorney sends you a client and you send them a personalized card thanking them, they will remember the gesture. When I receive a greeting card for the holidays or for my birthday from a fellow attorney, I am more likely to give them referrals as I will be reminded of them. If a client receives a birthday card from you, they will be happy.

One attorney that I spoke with told me he has gotten many referrals from clients after sending them a greeting card. There are now services that will mail cards from you automatically on preset dates. Obviously, you will have to pay for the cards and postage, but as the old adage goes, you have to spend money to make money.

The key to getting good letterhead and business cards is to find a good printer. I go to a little print shop that is owned by a friend. The prices are higher than a big box printer, but the work is better quality. You can find a quality printer in any town. A good printer will take the time to design the stationery with you and make sure that the final product turns out well. Again, remember you get what you pay for.

Websites are one of the most popular topics of discussion for attorneys. Like many topics that attorneys love to discuss, there are several schools of thought. Some attorneys, mostly older ones, will tell you that you do not need a website. These attorneys will tell you that there is nothing wrong with a phone. Some attorneys will tell you that in order to attract any new clients to your website, you have to spend a lot of money to make your website more visible and marketable. Opponents of websites will tell you that there are so many attorney websites that no one will ever find yours. This school of thought makes some valid points. For your website to come up first when someone searches on a type of law is incredibly expensive.

Google and other companies make fortunes off of Internet searches. For those that don't know how it works, the more you pay a search engine, the more visible your website becomes. If you are not paying a search engine, your website will come up on page 42,000 of the search results. If you are not paying to advertise your site, the only way anyone will find your site is if they either enter your exact address or search for the exact website name.

One of the other schools of thought swears by websites and will tell you how they receive large amounts of their clients off of the Internet. These attorneys will tell you that you must have a website and that every attorney needs one. I think an attorney should have a website, but not for the purposes of necessarily attracting clients.

I have had my website now for about two years. I have never gotten a client off the website, but I have had a lot of clients tell me that they were referred to me and checked out my website before deciding to hire me. I also have current clients that checked out my website to find out more about my practice. The front page of my website has about forty or so case results from the last couple of years. Clients have told me that they like the list because it shows I handle a lot of cases and have gotten good results.

There are a million ways to do a website and very few of them are wrong. I do caution young attorneys that it is better to not have a website than to have a bad website. A potential client will probably not be turned off if you do not have a website but may be turned off if you have a bad website. I have seen a lot of terrible websites. If you know how to design your own website, there is nothing wrong with doing it yourself. If you have no idea what you are doing and have no artistic ability, you should think about letting someone else design your website.

A professional web designer will charge thousands of dollars to design a website. Consider asking your friends to see if they know how to build a website. Be careful who you let mess with your website. I had a friend who told me he knew what he was doing, and then my email stopped working for three days. If you don't have a friend that can *competently* build you a website, consider contacting the local art college or design school and seeing if a student will do it for a couple hundred bucks. As far as hosting the website is concerned, companies like Go Daddy will host a simple site for $10 to $20 a year.

Business Bank Accounts

You must have at least one business account. The money in that account should only be for and from the business. Never deposit money from the business into your private account. There are several reasons not to do this, and one of them is for tax purposes. If you are audited, you do not want to have to explain to the I.R.S. why you deposited business money into a personal account or vice versa. Many banks have free business accounts. There is no reason for you to be paying the bank to have the account. Many banks want you to open your business account at their bank, so you should ask what incentives the bank offers for new accounts. The incentives can be anything from a free safe deposit box to a couple hundred dollars in cash.

Make sure you know what the rules are in your state for attorney trust accounts. An attorney trust account is one in which an attorney must deposit money that belongs to the client or that is not yet earned by the attorney. Even though the money is in the attorney's account, it belongs to the client. Many states do not require attorneys to have trust accounts, but some do. For example, in Arizona, a client's money that is not yet earned must go into something called an IOLTA account. IOLTA stands for Interest On Lawyers Trust Accounts. The interest from these accounts does not go to the client or the attorney but instead goes to a charitable organization fund run by the state bar.

Rules for maintaining trust accounts are very complicated. Many attorneys get themselves in trouble for not properly maintaining the accounts because they do not follow the rules. In Arizona, every year, a number of attorneys get themselves in trouble with the bar by either comingling funds or not properly keeping records of the account. Make sure you check the rules for your state and learn them. Often, state bars will offer continuing legal education classes on maintaining a trust account. If you are not required have to have a trust account, I would recommend you not have one. I do not have one, as I only do criminal defense work and my fees are earned upon receipt.

TECHNOLOGY

Technology is one of the few places where a new attorney can have an advantage over an older, more experienced attorney. Chances are a new attorney will be more comfortable with technological advances and will be more likely to use the technology. I recently had an older attorney ask me if I knew what PowerPoint was and how it worked. I have been using PowerPoint for presentations since high school. He had more experience than me, but he didn't know what PowerPoint was. Using technological advances in your practice can give you an advantage, make your life easier, and make your practice run smoother. One of the biggest advances in technology in the last couple of years has been smartphones.

Today, from my phone, I can check my schedule, pull up a file, check a court docket, deposit a check, see who owes me money, or scan a document. Even a couple of years ago, many of these technologies did not exist. I am sure that two years from now my phone will be able to do things that I can't even imagine today. New attorneys should become familiar and comfortable with all the things their phones can do. Here are a few basic suggestions for getting the most out of your phone.

You must have a smartphone. Your smartphone must be hooked up to your email. When a court or potential client is trying to reach you by email, you must be available. If you are only getting emails at your office, you will likely miss out on opportunities. Also, look into the number of providers that allow you to swipe a credit card from your phone. This is a great technology as it allows you to take payment without being at your office. New amazing smartphone programs continue to come out and you should use these programs to your advantage. I believe that pretty much a whole practice can now be run from a smartphone.

One other form of technology that you must have is some sort of backup data storage. Many of the important documents you will have will be on your computer. Not only will your computer contain documents but it will also contain motions, filings, pleadings, and many other things you do not want to lose. There are many options for data storage. There are traditional flash drives or external hard drives. There is nothing wrong with these devices, but if you use them, make sure you store them in a different place than your computer. If there is a fire at your office and your computer is next to your external hard drive, you will still lose everything.

Today, there are more data storage options that store information in off-site data centers. Many of these services are referred to as the "cloud" because your information is stored in a figurative cloud. I prefer off-site services because the data is always in a different place than your computer, so they cannot both be destroyed at the same time. There are a number of companies that charge you a monthly or yearly fee to store your data. I prefer a free service called Dropbox. The program allows you store up to several gigs of data for free. If you want more storage, you can add more for a fee. With the program, I can access files from any computer and from my smartphone. I can be sitting in court without my laptop and pull up any file that I have saved in my dropbox. The bottom line is, one way or another, you must back up your data.

Another potentially useful technology is software designed for certain types of practices. I say potentially useful because you have to make sure the benefit outweighs the cost. If you will use the software, and it will make you money, than think about buying it. There are many different programs for attorneys. Some of the programs are designed to help with billing and trial prep. Some programs are designed for bankruptcy attorneys or immigration attorneys. I know both immigration attorneys and bankruptcy attorneys that would have a hard time functioning without their respective software.

At first, you will probably won't have the money for any software. Once you can afford the software, you must seriously ask yourself if you actually need it or if it is just something cool that you kind of want. Remember that when you are starting out, managing your expenses will determine if your practice sinks or swims. Once you decide you need the software, buy the best program that is available on the market. Talk to other attorneys in your field and they will tell you what program is best. I know that for bankruptcy attorneys, there is one software program is that a lot better than its competition. Like most quality products, this particular program costs more than the cheap knockoffs. One attorney told me they tried the cheaper program to save money. They told me the cheap program was so terrible that the money savings were not worth it.

The main lesson with technology is that it is always evolving and new and better products are always coming out. I am sure that by the time you are reading this there will be new technology out that will make our lives easier and save us time. Learning how to use new technology can be difficult, but it must be done. I know many attorneys that still use WordPerfect and never learned Word. One problem they are now having is that they are not able to file some documents with courts as the documents have to be created in Word. The point is that attorneys must stay on top of new technologies.

When you start your own practice you will start getting calls from legal research providers. Westlaw and Lexis are the two biggest companies, but there are others. In general, I suggest you avoid subscribing to the services for several reasons. The first reason is cost. The services are incredibly expensive and generally not worth the price. With most of the services, you can reduce the cost by paying for limited access. If you are practicing bankruptcy law in New York, you do not need access to maritime cases from Holland. The services will try to sign you to a multi-year contract, which can really add up over time.

The second reason I suggest avoiding "pay for use" services is because you can usually find places to do research for free. Most cities will have legal libraries that are free to use. When I started my practice, I would often do legal research at one of the downtown courthouses. I had free access to Westlaw and made good use of it. Another good place to find free Westlaw or another service is at your law school. Even if you have graduated, most law schools will still let you use the library. Even if you are not close to your law school, you may be able to use the local law school for research. Many law schools will allow local attorneys to use their legal library.

If you are sharing an office with other attorneys, ask if you can pay them to use their on-line research provider. With the permission of the provider, you may be able to get your own account for cheaper than it would be to buy your own account. Always remember that your biggest task is to find ways to save money.

MOTIONS

As most of you know, a motion is a written request to the court. The motion can address something very simple like a Notice of Appearance. Motions can also address substantive matters like a Motion to Suppress or a Motion For a Directed Verdict. Motions, like all attorney work, should be done with a great degree of care and thought. You should never turn in a motion that you have not had someone read over for grammar and typo mistakes. You do not want a judge reading your motion and noticing that you confused than and then or don't know how to capitalize words correctly.

Depending on the type of practice you have, you may be writing many motions. For example, personal injury and criminal defense attorneys will write more motions than estate-planning attorneys. Some attorneys build an entire practice of motion writing. Attorneys who do post-conviction work or appeals work spend most of their time writing motions. Writing motions, like everything else, becomes easier with practice. When writing motions, there is no substitution for experience, which comes with repetition. The first time I wrote a suppression motion it took me a lot more time than it takes me to write one now.

One of the keys to writing good motions is to remember that the wheel has already been invented. New attorneys must remember that there is nothing wrong with building off of someone else's motion. I will often talk to a fellow defense attorney and ask them if they have a motion that I can use. I can save myself a lot of time by building my motion off of someone else's. In criminal defense, a lot of the same issues come up, so why reinvent the wheel? If I know that a friend of mine has a perfect motion for my probable cause issue, why write my own from scratch?

Never use someone else's motion without their permission as that would be plagiarism and very unprofessional. When borrowing someone else's motion, make sure you make all the necessary changes. I once got to watch a video of a judge screaming at a defense attorney who used someone else's motion and forgot to make the necessary changes. The defense attorney forgot to change "she" to "he" and made other obvious mistakes. Judges are okay with your motion building on someone else's, but they also want you to put the time in to make it correct.

Over time, you will develop your own motion bank that will make your life easier. Every time you write a motion, you should save it for future use. For example, I have a section in my own motion bank for Notice of Appearance Motions for different courts. I have one for each of the municipal courts, Justice of the Peace courts, and Superior Court. Every time I have to file a Notice of Appearance, having the old motions saves me time as I only have to change the dates and the defendant's name. The more motions you have in your motion bank, the easier your life will be.

EXPANDING: IS BIGGER BETTER?

At some point, you will have to decide if you want to expand your practice. If you do expand, you will also have to decide how big and how fast you want to grow. Many attorneys want to grow their practices because they want to make more money. Other attorneys want to make their practices bigger so that the firm appears more prestigious. New attorneys must remember that there are perils to growing your practice. The first thing that new attorneys must think about is that a bigger firm doesn't mean a more profitable firm. A larger firm may take in more money, but that doesn't mean it is netting more of a profit. Many firms learn this the hard way when it is too late. Consider the following hypothetical.

The Smith Law Firm is run by one attorney. The attorney wants to expand her practice, so she hires two new paralegals and two associate attorneys. Ms. Smith goes out and spends a lot of money on advertising and the clients start coming and everyone is happy. All is good for a couple of months, but then the clients slow down. The advertising bills are still due, the salaries of the new employees must be paid, and soon Ms. Smith is out of money. The bigger your practice, the more balls you are juggling.

Even if the clients don't stop coming, Ms. Smith has still increased her overhead when she added the new employees. Ms. Smith may be grossing more profit, but when you subtract all the new expenses, she may actually be making less money than she was before. Remember that just because you have more clients, it doesn't necessarily mean you are netting more of a profit.

The other thing that new attorneys must remember about expanding their practices is that the bigger the firm, the more problems you will have to deal with. When you have no employees, you don't have employee problems to deal with. When you have one employee, you have one set of problems. When you have three employees, you have three sets of problems. Instead of worrying about payroll, showing up late, insurance, workers comp, attitude issues, and other problems for one person, you now have to worry about those issues for three different people.

My point is not that expansion is bad. My point is that if you do decide to expand, first make sure it makes financial sense. Done correctly, expanding can net more of a profit. Also, make sure you are prepared to handle all the headaches that come with having an employee and that you absolutely need that employee. Right now I am busy enough that I could employ an assistant, but I chose not to. The reason I choose not to have an assistant is because I prefer to keep the money that I would be paying my assistant for myself.

If you do choose to expand, you need to decide what kind of vision you have for your growing practice. There are several different models that can be built. I have equated the type of firm with restaurants because it illustrates my point. It should go without saying that my descriptions generalize. There are excellent large firms and terrible small firms, so size can be deceptive. As with everything in our profession, there are always exceptions.

The first type of practice is the fast food model. The fast food law firm model is high quantity, low quality. These types of firms depend on high-volume advertising. The firms are dependent on advertising as they get virtually no referrals because their clients are generally dissatisfied with the quality of their work. The firms are usually large and can have anywhere from ten to thirty or more attorneys. In general, these firms are an embarrassment to the legal profession. Often, these firms will advertise very low prices to get people in the door.

Once a potential client is in the door, the firm uses a lot of high-pressure sales techniques. I have heard of some people taking a potential client's ID and not giving it back until the potential client signs up. If you have ever been to a time-share sales presentation, you get the idea. This type of practice is often attractive to attorneys because they can make a lot of money. The practice can be very profitable because of the large volume of clients that come to the firm. The large amount of money is made at the expense of reputation, but some attorneys are okay with this trade off. Unfortunately, more and more of these firms are popping up in the fields of criminal defense, personal injury, bankruptcy, and immigration.

The next type of law firm model is the national sit-down dinner restaurant model. The food is not great, but not terrible. The restaurants have a lot of locations and the service is usually okay. The service at these firms is often very middle-of-the-road. This type of firm does not rip off consumers, but does very mediocre work. This model of practice is also often dependent on advertising. A firm using this model will have a number of attorneys and may expand or contract as need be. These types of firms can also be very profitable because of the large volume of clients.

Another type of law firm model is the small, expensive steak house model. The restaurants have excellent service and excellent food. These firms generally only have a few attorneys and do excellent work for a high price. Generally, experienced attorneys that have built up their reputation run these firms and now have potential clients come to them through referrals. These practices spend very little money on advertising and can be selective about the clients they want. If you do want employees or associate attorneys, this is the type of practice you want to have. This model has the best of both worlds. You can still have other attorneys making money for you, but the practice is small enough so you can make sure that the work being performed is up to your standards.

The last type of law firm is the hole-in-the-wall restaurant that has won every culinary award and has an eight-month wait list. Solo attorneys usually run these practices. The attorneys that run these practices are often the best of the best and charge the most money. The attorneys running the practices are very selective about the clients they pick. The attorney is able to devote more attention to each client as they have fewer clients, but each client pays a lot. I cannot think of one of these attorneys that I know that has been in practice for less than thirty years.

HIRING STAFF

When you are ready to hire an employee, there are a number of factors you must think about. One of the first things you need to think about is how much you will pay your new employee. Obviously, the more you pay, the more experienced and qualified candidates you will get. If you are looking for a paralegal or assistant and you are offering to pay minimum wage, you will get minimum wage applicants. When deciding how much to pay a new employee, talk to other attorneys and ask what they are paying. Once you know what other attorneys are paying their staff, you will have a better idea what to pay yours.

The next factor you must consider is what type of personality you want your new employee to have. Do you want someone who is very talkative, or quite? Someone who is introverted, or outgoing? If you are very outgoing, you may not want an employee who is the same way. The point is that you must think about the traits you want in an employee before you hire someone. Like every part of running a practice, deciding on the type of employee you want takes preparation and planning. Once you know how much you will be paying and what traits you want in an employee, you will have to conduct interviews.

Interviews are a great way to learn about someone but remember that they are like first dates. The person you are interviewing is putting on a show for you and trying to impress you. Interviewing someone is not enough. You must get references. If someone doesn't have references, this is a red flag. Once you hire someone, you must immediately be clear with them what your expectations are. If you want your employees dressed a certain way or to mark files a certain way, you must tell them this. If you expect your employee to be on time and not five minutes late every day, this must also be made clear to them. The more you communicate your expectations, the better the chances that the employee will do what you ask.

CHAPTER 11
WHAT NO ONE TOLD YOU IN LAW SCHOOL (BUT SHOULD HAVE)

A LOT MORE GRAY IN REAL LIFE

One of the major differences between being in law school and actually practicing is the amount of gray. In law school, there is a lot more black and white and right and wrong. When you begin to practice you see that answers are rarely clear cut. In law school there is always a right answer. Whether it be in class on an exam or a quiz, most of the time the professor will say there is a correct answer. If it's in contracts class, the professor will say if a contract has been formed. If the question is in torts, the professor will tell you if an intentional tort has been committed. Obviously, there are gray areas in law school, but there is a lot more gray in actual practice.

Just one example of how things are less black and white in actual practice is how judges rule on motions and evidentiary issues. When you are in law school, the judge in casebooks always makes the right decision. If something is not admissible under the rules of evidence, the judge makes the right call. If a search violated the fourth amendment, the judge suppresses the evidence. In real practice, judges do not always make the right call. Sometimes judges make the wrong call because they don't understand the law or sometimes they do not like you or the defendant. In real life, judges are people and they make mistakes. Talk to any practicing attorney and they will tell you stories of judges making mistakes. This is not to say that judges normally get things wrong, because that would not be fair. Judges try to do a good job and get most things correct, but not always.

THERE IS NO SAFETY NET

When you are a practicing attorney, there is no safety net. If you make a serious mistake you can be sued, suspended, or even disbarred. I don't say this to scare new attorneys. I say this so that new attorneys are careful and do not get themselves in trouble. When you are in law school, even if you fail a class, you can retake it. In practice, you are usually not given a chance to fix a mistake.

In law school, there is a greater support system than in practice. In law school there are guidance counselors, tutors, deans, and other people that can help. In practice, attorneys are often on their own. As long as new attorneys understand this at the beginning, they can plan accordingly. Attorneys must go out and find people to help them and mentor them. New attorneys should understand that they must build their own support system where they can turn for guidance.

CLIENTS GENERALLY DO NOT CARE WHERE YOU WENT TO SCHOOL

In law school, there is a lot of focus on law school rankings and what tier your school is in. In general, clients don't care about where you went to school. Clients care about results and if you can help them. Also, where you went to law school will not dictate your success or failure in the legal profession. If you went to a super prestigious law school, this does not guarantee success. If you went to the lowest ranked law school in the country, you can still become a world-class attorney. What will dictate your success or failure is your ability to work hard and learn. In four years of practice, I have had exactly one defendant ask me where I went to law school. The defendant was court-appointed and homeless. New attorneys that did not go to prestigious top-tier law schools must remember that they can be just as competent as any famous law school attorney.

People in the legal community know which attorneys are competent and which are not. When I talk to my attorney friends, none of us have ever said: "She is a wildly incompetent attorney but she went to a super good big-name law school so she is still a good attorney." I know plenty of terrible attorneys that went to big name law schools. I also know some excellent attorneys that went to fourth-tier law schools.

When clients walk into your office, they may be impressed by your law school but they will be a lot more impressed by your reputation and your competence. Every criminal defense client would rather have an attorney that went to a no-name law school but got their buddy out of prison than a Harvard grad that doesn't know where the criminal court is. I really believe even corporate clients at big prestigious law firms would rather have a competent attorney than a weak attorney who went to a prestigious law school. Do not let where you went to school dictate your mindset.

LIKABLE > KNOWLEDGEABLE

If you asked most law students if it is more important for an attorney to be likeable or knowledgeable, they will say knowledgeable. If you ask most practice attorneys the same question, they will tell you the opposite. Obviously, the best attorneys are likable and knowledgeable, but many attorneys are one and not the other. An attorney that is knowledgeable but not likeable will have a hard time making a living as they will have a hard time getting clients. They will also have a hard time dealing with other attorneys and judges.

An attorney that is likable only will probably have a more profitable career than a knowledgeable, non-likable attorney.

Clients want to like their attorneys. I have seen many criminal defense attorneys build profitable practices while knowing very little of the law. The reason these attorneys can build profitable practices is because they are able to get clients and the clients refer other clients to them because they like them. I also know attorneys that are incredibly knowledgeable on the law but can hardly make a living as no one wants to hire them. My point is not to tell people that knowledge is not important, because it is. My point is that new attorneys must understand that they must be likeable not only for clients, but for other attorneys and judges.

A FRIGHTENING NUMBER OF INCOMPETENT ATTORNEYS

There are an amazing number of incompetent attorneys. Some are lazy, some have substance abuse issues, some are burnt out, and some were never very good attorneys to start with. There are incompetent people in every profession, and attorneys are no different. Just as there are bad plumbers, nurses, roofers, or gardeners, there are bad attorneys. New attorneys need to know that there are bad attorneys for several reasons. The problem with an incompetent attorney is the great amount of damage they can do. An incompetent attorney can get an innocent person sent to prison, cost someone their life savings, or at the least, hurt the reputation of the legal profession.

No matter what field of law you are in, you will have to deal with bad attorneys. If you are a prosecutor, you will have to deal with incompetent defense attorneys. If you are a civil attorney, you will have to deal with incompetent opposing counsel. New attorneys must be prepared for the reality that they will deal with attorneys that have no idea what they are talking about. If you are a new attorney and your opposing counsel is incompetent, the sooner you realize that he is incompetent, the better off you will be. A new attorney must never assume that just because someone is an attorney he is automatically competent.

New attorneys must understand that it is up to them to repair the reputational harm of attorneys caused by incompetent attorneys. New attorneys must always remember that they are representatives of a profession and must do everything in their power to present that profession in the best light possible. Every time a new attorney is competent and does the right thing, this helps the reputation of attorneys.

There are not only an amazing number of incompetent attorneys, but there are an amazing number of incompetent professionals everywhere. From judges to support staff, there are a lot of people who are not good at their jobs. Some are lazy, while others have a lack of training. For every competent judge and support person in the court, there is someone who has no idea what they are doing. I have had to deal with bailiffs and clerks in many different courts that have made all kinds of mistakes, ranging from big to small. I have had clerks set trials on the same days, forget to give defendants their paper work, and lose entire court files. Again, the legal profession is no different than any profession in this regard.

MANAGING STUDENT LOANS

There are some things you can do to prepare for the repayment of your loans while you are still in law school. One of the keys to dealing with lenders is to be proactive. If your loans go into default, you will have fewer options than if you would have dealt with them sooner.

One way to be proactive is to contact your providers and ask them about different repayment programs. You will need to do your homework and learn about the different programs. With some of the programs the interest is paused, while with others the interest continues to accrue but you do not have to make regular payments. If your loans are with different providers, you may want to look into consolidating your loans. If your loans are consolidated, you may be able to get a better interest rate. Another advantage of consolidation is that if your loans are all in one place, it is easier to know what is going on with them.

Most of your loans will have some kind of grace period after you graduate. Depending on the type of loan and lender, the grace period can be from six months to a year. Get all the details from the lender and take full advantage of any grace periods that are offered. Once you do have to pay back the loans, ask about what type of income-based repayment options are offered. Income based repayment programs are exactly what they sound like. Every year, you submit financial documents to your lender and they work out a new payment amount. The big advantage of the income-based program is that your monthly payments will be a lot lower than on the traditional repayment plan.

I can't stress how important it is that you stay on top of your student loans. The loan provider companies are like the Motor Vehicle Department. If they can screw something up, they will. While working on this section, I thought I should check on my income-based repayment application that I have to resubmit every year. After twenty minutes on hold, I found out that Sallie Mae has processed my application too early (I didn't know that could be done). Long story short, I straightened everything out. If I had not called them today, my whole income-based repayment program would have been messed up for the whole year, and it would have cost me a lot of money and a lot of stress.

There is no worse feeling than when your lenders are calling you and telling you that you owe more money than you have. I have had many friends that were not able to make their payments because they failed to plan. Ideally, you should start planning on how you will manage your loans before you graduate. Burying your head in the sand and avoiding the issue will not help. The longer you put off making arrangements to pay, the worse off you will be. No one hates dealing with lenders more than I do, but it is simply something that must be done. You must stay on top of your loans.

MANY ATTORNEYS NEVER MAKE A LOT OF MONEY

There are several reasons why there is a perception that all attorneys are rich. One cause of this is that there are some attorneys that make huge amounts of money. There are partners at huge firms that make insane amounts of money. Another reason I think the perception exists is that many attorneys like to pretend they have a lot of money. The last reason I think that the perception exists, is due to the popular media. Films like *The*

Firm show law school graduates being offered huge paychecks upon graduation. The reality is often very different for attorneys.

A huge number of attorneys live paycheck to paycheck. No doubt some of this is because of their own poor planning. As discussed, if you do not manage your money, you will have no money. Many attorneys are not bad with money but simply do not earn a lot. Some attorneys do not earn very much because they work for the government. Many government agencies currently have pay increase freezes due to budget cuts. What this means for attorneys working in those offices is that they cannot get a pay increase even if they deserve it.

Many private attorneys don't make a lot of money for a different reason. As discussed, there are more and more attorneys competing for the same clients. Attracting private clients may mean spending a lot of advertising. Many private attorneys simply do not have the money to advertise. Some private attorneys are able to rely on referrals for clients but not all can. Many clients will speak to four or five attorneys before picking one. This tells me that there is more supply than demand. It is important that new attorneys understand that many attorneys never make a lot of money.

CHAPTER 12
QUALITY OF LIFE ISSUES

"The job will not save you." *–Lester Freamon, The Wire-*

I will be honest with you. There are a lot of unhappy attorneys. When you are in law school this is not something you are told, but it is something that you need to know. One source of attorneys not being as happy as they want to be is the idea that they are not making enough money. Like everything, there is a positive and a negative way to look at your income.

You will only be as happy as your expectations. In other words, happiness is relative. If you expect to make millions and you make less than that, you will not be happy. The idea works both ways. If you expect to make $40,000 and you make $50,000, you will be thrilled. Guess how much I made in my first year of practice? I made barely over $20,000 for the year. I didn't make a lot, but I was thrilled. I had made more than zero and I made enough to pay the bills and go forward to my second year. If I had started my practice thinking that if I made less than $30,000 I would be disappointed and angry, that's exactly what would have happened. How much money you make has to be seen in perspective

Perspective is the key to many things in life. One of my favorite TV shows is *Deadliest Journeys*. The show follows people around the world with dangerous jobs. One episode features sulfur miners in Indonesia. The miners walk up the side of a volcano carrying hundreds of pounds of sulfur on their back. The miners go up the side of the volcano in flip-flops because those are the only shoes they can afford. Most of the miners die around forty years of age from breathing the fumes.

Earlier I said I made *only* $20,000 my first year. The sulfur miners will not make $20,000 in their entire lives. This is perspective. A large part of your happiness or unhappiness in the legal profession will depend on your outlook. If you think about how fortunate you are to not have to be a sulfur miner in Indonesia, you will be happier. If you think about how you are not making as much as another attorney, you will be less happy. Simple but true. Worrying about money is one source of attorney unhappiness. Not appreciating their jobs is another source of unhappiness.

Many attorneys would be happier if they remembered how lucky they are to be attorneys. Remember what percentage of the world would love to do what attorneys get to do. How many people wish they had a job where they got to dress up, sit in an air-conditioned office, and give advice to people. This is one way to look at what attorneys do. This is mostly my approach, and it helps me to keep things in perspective. Other attorneys have a different outlook. They complain about not making enough money, about hating their clients, about other things they do not like, and they end up unhappy. You will have to decide what your outlook is. Your outlook will have a huge effect on how happy you are in the legal profession.

The last major cause of unhappiness for attorneys worth discussing is burnout. It is important that you know there is a lot of burnout in the legal profession. Some attorneys get burned out on the work that they once loved. Other attorneys realize that they are doing work that they never wanted to do in the first place. Some attorneys get tired of the clients and just don't want to deal with them anymore.

I have seen a lot of attorney burnout, and it is not pretty. An attorney that is burnt out is constantly unhappy and constantly complaining. They are unhappy about their practice, their career, and pretty much everything. One attorney I know is so unhappy that other attorneys don't like to be around her. People don't get burnt out overnight. It happens slowly and usually takes months, if not years. Burnout doesn't have to be inevitable, and there are some things you can do to avoid burnout.

When you are young, try out different areas of law to see what you like and what you enjoy. Some young attorneys think they would hate criminal law, but when they try it they end up loving it. If you try an area of law and you hate it, that's okay, too. It is better to try something and realize that you don't like it than to never discover an area of law that you could have enjoyed. Think of this as when your mom made you eat some food you didn't want to and she told you that you just had to try it once.

Another good idea is to talk to attorneys that have been practicing for a while in the area of law you are interested in. You may think you may be interested in family law until you talk to some family law attorneys. The more attorneys you speak to, the better idea you will get if the field of law is for you. It is not a bad idea to attend some conferences for the field of law you are interested in. If you are interested in immigration law, find a local conference and go to it. This is a great way to meet many attorneys in one field of law all at once.

Something else that is very important to remember is that money will not make you happy. There is nothing wrong with wanting to make money. I believe it is easier to be comfortable with money than without. I have been very poor, and not being poor is better. Wanting to make money is different than thinking money will make you happy. Whenever a study or survey is done asking people what makes them happy, the answer is never money. The answer is always friends and family. I know lots of attorneys that make lots of money and are as far from happy as you can imagine. If you are unhappy without money, you will be unhappy with money. I think money can make a happy person happier, but money can't make an unhappy person happy.

"More money more problems . . . more problems more money" –*Young Jeezy*-

A young attorney must also remember that the more work you take on, the more stress you will have. There is nothing wrong with taking on a lot of work, but you must be aware that this will create more stress and more headaches. Your goal should be to find a good balance between making the amount of money you want and having the amount of stress you can handle. If you have too much stress, this is not good. If you do not have enough work, this will also lead to stress. As in most things in life, balance is key.

As many people know, one of the best ways to relieve stress is with exercise. You don't have to be a marathon runner to get exercise. Take fifteen minutes and walk around your office building or take your dog for a walk. It is not important what you do for exercise or how strenuous it is. As long as you are doing anything that involves moving, there will be a benefit. Getting exercise is not only good for your stress level but you will have more energy and be able to work more. Exercising is important, and so is taking time off.

Young attorneys must remember to take time off work. Make time for family, vacations, social outings, and anything else that you enjoy. Obviously, when you are starting out you will be taking fewer vacations and days off than you will be able to take when you are established, but you must make time for yourself. If you do not make time for yourself, you will get burned out. The entire point of having your own practice is to be able to enjoy things more and do things on your own schedule.

I started this chapter with a quote from one of my favorite TV shows, *The Wire*. The quote is being said to a detective that is obsessed with his work and willing to go to all ends to get the bad guy. The wise detective friend tells him that, "the job will not save him."

What the quote means is that people need to have more in their lives than work. No matter how good you are at your job, no matter how busy you are, you must have more than work. Work can bring you happiness, but not on the same level as family and friends. You need hobbies, families, activities, volunteer causes, and things you care about besides work. I have seen attorneys that have nothing in their lives aside from work and it is not something to aspire to. You must have balance. Work hard; spend a lot of time working, but have balance.

I have attorney friends that find balance in different ways. I have one attorney friend who has a condo in San Diego and drives there a couple times a month. I have friends that have cabins that spend as much time there as possible. Other attorneys stay in town but volunteer a lot at animal shelters or other worthy causes. I have one attorney friend who spends every weekend at various shelters trying to find homes for abandoned animals. For her, there is no better way to spend the weekend. I like to travel and try to have date night with my wife every Saturday. For me, having planned trips is important because it gives me something big to look forward to. It doesn't matter what you do to get away from work, but there has to be more to your life than work.

I know parts of this book may not be exactly optimistic, but I feel it is better that you start thinking about these issues that many attorneys neglect. In all honesty, the practice of law has been amazing to me. I have been able to do amazing things and make a good living in the process. For all of the complaining about difficult clients and the other problems in the legal profession, there is truly nothing else I would rather do. I have tried to follow all of the rules in the book. So far, the practice of law has been good to me and I hope it is for you also. If anything in this book is useful to you in your legal careers, I will be happy.

BEST OF LUCK!

INDEX

Made in the USA
Lexington, KY
20 July 2015